TWELFTH NIGHT
a screenplay

Trevor Nunn was educated at Downing College, Cambridge and in 1962 he won an ABC Director's Scholarship to the Belgrade Theatre, Coventry, where, as Resident Director, his productions included *The Caucasian Chalk Circle*, *Peer Gynt* and a musical version of *Around the World in Eighty Days*. In 1964, he joined the Royal Shakespeare Company, was made an Associate Director in 1965, and became the company's youngest ever Artistic Director in 1968. He was responsible for running the RSC until he retired from his post in 1986. His productions for the RSC included *The Revenger's Tragedy*, *The Relapse*, *The Alchemist*, *Henry V*, *The Taming of the Shrew*, *King Lear*, *Much Ado About Nothing*, *The Winter's Tale*, *Henry VIII*, *Hamlet*, *Macbeth*, *Antony and Cleopatra*, *Coriolanus*, *Julius Caesar*, *Titus Andronicus*, *Romeo and Juliet*, *The Comedy of Errors*, *As You Like It*, *All's Well That Ends Well*, *Once in a Lifetime*, *Three Sisters*, *Juno and the Paycock*, *Othello* (the final production at the Other Place) and *The Blue Angel* and *Measure for Measure* (the first two productions in the new Other Place). With his colleague, John Caird, he co-directed *Nicholas Nickleby* (winner of five Tony Awards), *Peter Pan* and *Les Miserables* which won eight Tony Awards and has become the most performed musical in the world. In 1982, he opened the RSC's new London home, the Barbican Theatre, with his production of Shakespeare's *Henry IV, Parts I and II*. 1986 saw the opening of the Swan Theatre in Stratford-upon-Avon which he conceived and for which he directed one of the first productions, *The Fair Maid of the West*. Outside the RSC, he has directed the Tony Award-winning *Cats*, *Starlight Express*, *Aspects of Love* and *Sunset Boulevard* for Andrew Lloyd Webber; *Chess*, *The Baker's Wife*, *Timon of Athens*, *Heartbreak House* and *Arcadia*. At Glyndebourne he has directed *Idomeneo*, *Porgy and Bess*, *Così fan tutte* and *Peter Grimes*; and at the Royal Opera House, *Porgy and Bess* (revival) and *Katya Kabanova*. His television work includes *Antony and Cleopatra* (BAFTA Award), *The Comedy of Errors*, *Macbeth*, *Three Sisters*, *Nicholas Nickleby* (Emmy Award), *Word of Mouth*, *Othello* and *Porgy and Bess*. He has directed three films, *Hedda*, *Lady Jane* and *Twelfth Night*. He is the Artistic Director (Designate) of the Royal National Theatre.

for a complete catalogue of Methuen Drama titles write to:

Methuen Drama
Random House
20 Vauxhall Bridge Road
London SW1V 2SA

William Shakespeare's

TWELFTH NIGHT

a screenplay by
Trevor Nunn

Methuen Film
in association with
Renaissance Film

A METHUEN SCREENPLAY

2 4 6 8 10 9 7 5 3

First published in Great Britain in 1996
by Methuen Drama
Random House, 20 Vauxhall Bridge Road,
London SW1V 2SA
and Australia, New Zealand and South Africa

Random House UK Limited Reg. No. 954009

A CIP catalogue record for this book
is available from the British Library

ISBN 0 413 71280 X

Typeset in 10 on 13.5 point Plantin Light
by Wilmaset Ltd, Birkenhead, Wirral
Printed in Great Britain
by Cox & Wyman Ltd, Reading, Berkshire

INTRODUCTION

Twelfth Night is one of the most enduringly popular of Shakespeare's plays in Britain, to the point where in my day at Royal Shakespeare Company scheduling meetings it was known as a 'banker', but it is curiously much less well known in America.

Perhaps it is the title itself that causes some resistance. After all, what does that title mean? What should anybody expect the work to be about when they see the title advertised?

Several memoranda I received discussing the play as a film project referred to it as 'Twelfth Knight' (presumably a distant sequel to Richard Gere as Sir Lancelot), and in one hasty fax I saw it titled as 'Twelve Nights', suggesting an even pacier and far more torrid version of *9½ Weeks*.

But mix-ups are understandable. You can search the text of Shakespeare's play from cover to cover and find no reference to Christmas or any other traditional context of the term 'Twelfth Night' and unlike *Measure for Measure* or *All's Well That Ends Well* there are no textual explanations of what bearing this proverbial-sounding title has on the work.

The explanation, superbly researched in Leslie Hotson's formative book, *The First Night of Twelfth Night*, is simply that Shakespeare's theatre company were commissioned to provide an entertainment for the Twelfth Night celebrations after the Christmas of 1602. Just as a modern theatre group might refer to a future project as the 'Homeless Benefit Sunday Night', or the 'Mid-Summer Revue', Shakespeare's group knew their new piece as 'The Twelfth Night Show' which became abbreviated to *Twelfth Night*. It was finally given a title, *What You Will*, in the same light-hearted category as *Much Ado About Nothing* or *As You Like It* and, I am certain, would have been advertised to that first-night audience as *What You Will* – but, let's face it, it's not much more helpful.

It is too late, nearly four hundred years later, to start a campaign to reinstate *What You Will* as the real title. But it is an equally insoluble conundrum when discerning film producers say that the disconnection between title and content is a serious disinclination to investing in the work.

Tom Stoppard suggested to me the problem of the title could be solved with a publicity campaign built around the slogan 'For eleven nights there was nothing, but then ... '.

For my part, I remembered back to meetings when colleagues were attempting to dissuade me from retaining the title *Les Miserables* at the time when, for the Royal Shakespeare Company, I first presented the musical based on Victor Hugo's great novel. 'Call it "The Outcasts" or "The Dispossessed" or "The Wretched",' people said. 'You can't have a musical with the word "miserable" in the title and you certainly can't have an unpronounceable phrase in a foreign language.' But the fact is, the title of Hugo's masterpiece had never been translated, it had always been known as *Les Miserables* since its first publication in English and therefore, I decided, the title had to be retained if anybody was to know that the stage musical was a version of this great epic work.

So, by that rule, *Twelfth Night* it had to be, despite the albatross weight of that phrase making the film possibility less buoyant than it might have been if I was able to call it 'Twin Trouble'.

It has become possible for many people to think in terms of filming Shakespeare almost entirely because of the achievement of Kenneth Branagh and his Renaissance Film Company in which he collaborated with producers David Parfitt and Stephen Evans. The breakthrough success of his *Henry V*, followed by the even bigger box-office success of his *Much Ado About Nothing* has made the film world, and Hollywood in particular, become interested again when, for years, everything concerning the Bard was darkness.

Early on in my formulation of the *Twelfth Night* film idea, Ken offered to share his experience with me, an action of quite extraordinary generosity and genuine concern for which I cannot adequately thank him. His advice was unerringly accurate. Everything that he told me to fear at that meeting eventually transpired; every device he suggested to deal with the disputes he predicted has, in the event, hugely helped to keep the film alive; he talked with the acquired wisdom of somebody much older – there was an absence of competitiveness – and this made me think all over again how thrilling it is to share in creative matters and how boring it is to allow the equally natural human urges of selfishness and ambition to turn artists inward.

He explained to me that the American market in particular would be opposed to identifying the writer as Shakespeare, because the name signalled to millions of potential viewers the unhappy hours they had spent during their education being forced to study something that seemed to be archaic and irrelevant. Shakespeare = turn-off.

All in all, then, that seemed to be quite a promising beginning – don't call it *Twelfth Night* and don't say it is by Shakespeare. In truth, I have every sympathy with the people whose job it is to market film product. They must frequently be pushed towards situations where to relinquish taste in order to achieve high box-office must be the preferred option, and they exist on their results. Everybody concerned with the making of a film wants it to reach the maximum possible audience, not because of money-earning considerations but because only by that means does their life-consuming effort, spread over many months to get the work to the screen, finally seem worth it. So who cares if that involves putting Shakespeare's name on the poster so small you couldn't read it at an eye test? – who cares if it's advertised as a wacky, slapstick fun-fest or as a sex-change shocker or as one sly suggestion had it, to solve any off-putting heavy classical impression, 'Shakespeare Lite'?

Ultimately, I suppose, nobody should care about such considerations if the integrity of the content of the film is not compromised. But then it has to be said, if you are unable to contemplate compromise, don't bother to start making a film. Compromise is called for in a myriad ways, for a myriad reasons – because of money, weather, schedule and these days rigorous methods of post-production testing whereby a director can be shown beyond dispute that what he has done, playing to a demographically researched and monitored audience, is not working. So why would I, a director whose experience has been more in the sheltered world of the theatre, choose to work in a form which could end up representing neither what I wanted nor Shakespeare? That question has a lengthy answer.

My relationship with *Twelfth Night* has amounted, for most of my working career, to a sad, eventful history, characterised by frustrations and unhappy accidents, resulting in me never getting to do my own theatre production of the text I most love.

At university, the excellent Waris Hussein (then Habibullah) beat me to the punch in proposing to stage it and I had to be content with playing Sebastian, twinned with the Viola of Margaret Drabble, soon to be an internationally revered novelist, in a student cast which also paraded the Belch of Ian McKellen and the Orsino of Corin Redgrave.

The intense pleasure of being involved in those performances of the play has made the memory precisely tangible, providing me some thirty years later with instant recall of our inflexions, extravagant physical business and the thrill of having spontaneous audience reaction becoming tumultuous as Shakespeare's plot thickens.

Early during my first professional job, I was asked by Anthony Richardson, the Artistic Director of the Belgrade Theatre in Coventry, if, given my student experience with Shakespeare and the Marlowe Society, I would be keen to direct something from the canon. My instant, if not reflex response, was to nominate *Twelfth*

Night but soon after I had begun preparations, I was informed that a director senior to me was unhappy about my queue jumping and I was urged to think of an alternative project for later in the year.

So once again I had to be content with being in somebody else's *Twelfth Night* – this time as Fabian – alongside an actor I greatly admired, called David Waller, as Belch. Waller had already opened my eyes and ears about Shakespeare when, several years earlier, I had been electrified by his astonishingly naturalistic, utterly believable Iago in the minute Ipswich Arts Theatre in my home town. Before that evening, Shakespeare for me had been synonymous with declamation and rhetoric and now suddenly, this turbulent, rule-breaking, unprecedentedly fast-thinking and fast-talking performance was overturning all previously received notions. The text was not being performed or 'spoken', it was being inhabited.

Even to be part of the same company as David Waller was luck enough for a twenty-two-year-old starting at the bottom of the haphazard pile, but to be sharing his scenes, observing at close quarters how he was able to convert uncertain direction into original insight through the filter of character and discussing with him his strand of the play and the furthest reaches of its meaning, was a gift from the theatre gods beyond calculable value.

My knowledge of the masterpiece was steadily increasing and the certainty of my assessment. It is one of those rare phenomena, the perfect work of art, like Mozart's *Figaro* or Billy Wilder's *Some Like it Hot*; but my jinx with the play took on yet more mysterious proportions when I joined the Royal Shakespeare Company and was tactfully dissuaded from my choice of *Twelfth Night* as the work with which to open my Shakespeare account, having won my spurs on Tourneur.

Years later, fascinated by the many stylized solutions to the play which seemed to abound (dodecahedron toting twins in mystical or divine androgyny, a Caroline romantic extravaganza, Illyria as a world of sunbaked Greek or Turkish adobe villages, Orsino as Narcissus) I still yearned to see Viola transforming herself into a boy out of emotional and social necessity; I still wanted her story to happen in a world where she would face real challenges and in which she would make real discoveries, about herself, about the prevailing assumptions of men towards her own gender and the constrictions upon her liberty that being a woman imposed.

But during this time, I saw the best stage production I have encountered (or expect to encounter) when Judi Dench played Viola with exquisite melancholy and her great comedienne's innate mischief, wherein Emrys James uncovered many levels of wry and caustic seriousness in his barefoot misfit Feste, and in which Donald Sinden was sublime in his grotesquely inflated vanity (I gratefully acknowledge that it was Donald who first corrected the sundial when he found God's chronometry in disagreement with his pocket-watch but such inspirations enter the folklore of the work and quite properly become common theatrical property).

This profound production in Stratford in 1969 was directed by John Barton, who had already exercised a mentor's influence on my development when, proposing that I should collaborate with him on a revival of *Henry V* in 1965, he educated me in his unique textual discipline, a finely-balanced mixture of scholarship, theatrical insight and common sense. Those weeks I spent working with John were indelible in their influence and invested me with a belief in collaboration as well as the beginnings of comprehending the limitlessly complex tool of Shakespeare's chosen form. John Barton's achievement and influence on generations of Shakespeare production has been every bit as momentous as the work of William Poel or Harley Granville Barker and deserves the equivalent fame.

John's production stressed that Illyria was, like Neverland or Shangri La or Prospero's Island, a magic place of the imagination operating according to its own rules so that it was unnecessary for contradictions to be explained or for farcical narrative extremes to be provided with social realistic justification; but drawing all disparate elements together was the omnipresent sea, audible in its ceaseless ebb and flow throughout and becoming the salve for all wounds, its 'salt waves fresh in love'.

There are of course as many valid productions of a masterpiece as there are imaginations to reflect its multifaceted density, so it is not surprising that I continued to feel that what I saw in the work had still to be released and that if I could ever get at it, the play would come out differently from previous versions. Ironically, I even found myself, in unforeseen crisis circumstances, rehearsing John Barton's production on tour in Australia and several years later, rehearsing an RSC touring version (with Ian McKellen as Toby Belch once again) directed by Jon Amiel who went on to become an internationally successful film director – but still nothing, however poor, that I could call my own.

When the Barbican Theatre was being pushed by financial extremity towards seasonal closure in 1989 after I had retired from the Company, I proposed that I should direct an 'all star' *Twelfth Night* to come to the aid of the strapped and beleaguered London RSC operation; but the plan failed to find favour and, for the umpteenth time, my own production had to go back into the box. Possibly born of this frustration and possibly in part realizing that the imagery that the play insistently provoked in my mind had always had a cinematic dimension, I started to think actively about making *Twelfth Night* into a film.

I have heard countless people enthuse that the best Shakespeare film they have ever seen is Kurasowa's *Throne of Blood*. Others argue that Kozintsev's Russian *Hamlet* claims pole position. Of course in Kurasowa's tingling and hypnotic movie, the spoken text could be written on the back of a postcard, and both films have screenplays that do not keep to Shakespeare's structure, and which cut the translated and reworked text to the point where it is secondary to action and image.

All films apart from the oddest wonderful exceptions (like Louis Malle's *My Dinner with Andre* or Eric Rohmer's *Claire's Knee*) subjugate the spoken word to action and image because quintessentially those are the priorities dictated by a hundred years of working experience with the moving photograph; so an English-language film version of a Shakespeare play begins with a massive and probably insoluble dilemma. The Shakespeare text is a masterpiece in itself, not a word of it is wasted or unattached to the dramatist's purpose and every loss of a line is not only a disservice to the writer but an occasion of pain and anguish to the director. But that same director knows that visual images do convey, and need to convey, a great deal of scenic and narrative information which it would be superfluous for the text to repeat; that cinematic construction is best served by scenes of brief impact, pushing the narrative forward at all times; that theatrical devices, such as soliloquy or asides, are not necessarily effective when translated to the screen; and that because large sums of money have to be invested before a film can happen at all then potential box-office return becomes the driving decision-making consideration, dictating necessities of length (or should I say brevity), speed, accessibility and the requirement that nothing be exclusive or esoteric.

So the English-language Shakespeare movie director is perpetually between Scylla and Charibdis hoping to find a channel through. Shakespeare, I imagine, encountered certain aspects of the same difficulty; in the prologue to *Romeo and Juliet* he refers to the 'two hours traffic of the stage' and yet regardless of whatever breakneck speed his text is spoken at, all the words of the published play cannot be crammed into one hundred and twenty minutes. So either the play was longer in performance than the prologue promised, or the playing text was cut down from the printed edition.

Perhaps the most fascinating of the textual conundrums lie in attempting to reconcile the different printed versions of *Hamlet*, which vary so greatly that it is not at all sure that any of them were played in their entirety. Least likely of all is that a conflation of the several texts was ever played or intended to be played by the dramatist. Nearer to our own time, J. M. Barrie wrote several different versions of *Peter Pan* prior to publication, including scenes for special occasions, plus a novelized expansion of the play and a film script, almost as if he didn't want to let go of it by giving it to a printer. He seemed to fear that the work would become 'finished' by an official publication. It is not impossible that Shakespeare had a similar relationship with his texts and attitude to publication, but since, to the best of our knowledge, he never supervised the printing of one of his plays we shall never know.

At all events, Shakespeare would surely have *disapproved* of the swingeing text-cutting that has characterized most films of his plays, including the massive number of central incidents and characters missing from both the famous Olivier *Hamlet* and *Richard III*, the swathes removed from Orson Welles's *Othello* and *Macbeth* and the textual remainders of the Brando/Gielgud *Julius Caesar* and the Max Reinhardt *A Midsummer Night's Dream*.

Before a film production company will look at the viability of any project, they have to be satisfied with the screenplay, never mind that the original author happens to be the greatest dramatist who has ever lived and without whom our notion of the limits of dramatic form would be a poor thing. So in pondering *Twelfth Night*, the movie, my first tack was to calculate how much text I could bear to dispense with while managing through descriptive notes and conceptual proselytizing, to make the 'script' a good read and a turn-on for potential film producers who wade through morasses of standardized material every week.

I failed. The first reactions I got were 'Too long, too difficult, too wordy and who is this supposed to be for?' From one executive, 'It's great, but can't we cut all the blah-blah?' Ouch. But then, a close friend of mine, the dramatist and screen-writer, Richard Nelson, with whom I had collaborated on the thrillingly composed musical *Chess* and with whom I was developing another film script, challenged me vigorously on the last point – who was *Twelfth Night* for? Richard was sure, if somewhat cynically sure, that knowing the genre or the *category* of film one was attempting to be in would be essential to the whole project and not just to marketing executives when it came to the selling campaign. I was chastened by his direct questioning but equally reminded that the categorizing of Shakespeare's plays in the First Folio into Tragedies, Comedies and Histories is almost arbitrary, and that the Elizabethan response to the term comedy was obviously more to do with tone and outcome than with counting the laughs. So deciding that *Twelfth Night* should be a teen pick or a date movie or this year's most unusual romantic comedy wouldn't serve the constant contrasts of style and emphasis of a work that defies summary and achieves the near impossible task of changing our reaction from laughter to tears over and over again.

Nevertheless, Richard did push me round the corner into considering the work as a film rather than as a photographed play and therefore, that it had to have a shape and a content that would owe nothing to a scholar's assumption that anyone watching it would have read it and seen it in many other versions before.

This reminded me of the dichotomy I faced at Stratford-upon-Avon, running and directing countless plays for the Royal Shakespeare Company, the world-famous theatre at the birthplace. Our audience frequently comprised the most extreme spectrum, some people familiar with the play, sitting alongside people who had not only never been to a Shakespeare before but in some cases never to a theatre; sitting alongside people who were teaching the play or had just written a book about it! So where did you pitch the performance? How did you unify such a disparately wide mix of audience?

The answer at Stratford was that a great deal of scholarship went into the preparation of our work, but finally our intention was to be as populist and accessible as we could manage short of betraying the text.

So resolving to make the film of *Twelfth Night* accessible was a congenial project for me, even though I discovered at every stage of the film-making that things that I thought were now as clear as crystal were stubbornly providing problems of comprehension for others. It was not so much individual lines and archaic words; it was the *reason* for things happening in the story. When you are used to a Shakespeare plot, you don't question it, but now I had to question everything.

The most important decisions were already made in my mind, and had been for years.

Twelfth Night is so emphatically about gender, that the presentation of it and the audience's awareness of it are crucial. It is the only work I know of that has as its central protagonists identical twins of opposite gender. Throughout dramatic literature, there are many mistaken identity comedies based on identicality from Plautus to *The Comedy of Errors* to *Ring Round the Moon* but always the gender of the twins is the same. Shakespeare's choice of a story about twins, one a boy, the other a girl, tells us precisely where his interest lies – how are men in love different from women in love; what is attractive to men about the male in women; what is attractive to women about the female in men; is love between two people of the same gender of the same kind as between people of opposite gender? So he invents a plot to provoke all these ideas, contriving to show us every facet of the comedy of gender with the parallel stories of Orsino's love for Olivia, Olivia's love for the boy we know to be Viola, Antonio's love for Sebastian, Viola's love for Orsino and Orsino's growing love for Viola who he knows as Cesario.

I wanted this story to happen in a society where the differences between men and women were at their greatest, when men were clothed to reveal their shape in trousers and boots and close-fitting waistcoats and jackets; and when conversely women were considered delicate, sensitive and decorative creatures, wearing clothing to hide and disguise them, and were reliant upon male strength and decorum to defend them.

Of course, pretty much every century except our own can provide examples of these social attitudes, but the last years of the previous century took those attitudes to extremes exemplified in the dress silhouettes of the two genders.

The second theme, much discussed by the protagonists and also affecting the second plot surrounding Malvolio, is 'disguise' in the sense of deception, and concealment and perhaps most important in the case of Olivia's puritanical steward, of hypocrisy. I not only wanted Viola's 'disguise' to be achieved at some effort from her and maintained under some tension – since Shakespeare so frequently plays with the idea that her cover is about to be blown – but also to accentuate the gender story. So I was interested in Viola (as Cesario) entering an exclusively male world at Orsino's castle, a military academy of a court wherein she is expected – to her alarm – to ride horses, sword fight at fencing practice, play billiards, smoke cigars, drink alcohol and generally wrestle and horseplay around, so that she finds out the hard way what it is to be 'one of the boys'.

To be blunt about it, I was most emphatically not interested in the page boy Viola I have often seen, cherubic with long, girly hair, padded doublet, codpiece, decorated pantaloons, heeled shoes and still enjoying the femininity of lace cuffs and ruffs. Such a Cesario I felt would be costing Viola very little, not confronting her with many challenges beyond her experience and therefore not liberating her from the over-protective view of women that has enveloped her.

These considerations began to shape this script which takes every opportunity to *show* these things as opposed to having them only referred to and which requires locations which can serve the fictional or fairy-tale elements of the story but still encourage the audience to believe that what is happening to Viola in disguise is real, as much as the social and moral infighting between Malvolio and Sir Toby and Malvolio and Feste is real.

To this end, I felt it was immensely important that audiences anywhere should be able to *recognize* the upstairs/downstairs hierarchy of Olivia's household, in which a metaphorical and actual green baize door separates the world of bibulous, aristocratic, irresponsible Sir Toby, with his vacuous, impressionable, aristocratic guest, Sir Andrew, from the butler, Malvolio, who rules the servants hall with a rod of iron and is beginning – according to the aristocrats – to get ideas above his station.

The clash is only partly one of class (and it would be uncomfortably narrow-minded if it were only that) because it derives just as much from the perception of Malvolio's hypocrisy – his phoney puritanism, his self-serving stance as a killjoy, which when it is articulated by the governess or lady's maid, Maria, leads to the plan to exploit his hubris, expose his sexual fantasies and unmask his disguise.

Shakespeare's prose scenes have an uncanny contemporary feel of real speech and, as their names suggest, Sir Toby, Sir Andrew and Mistress Mary are firmly rooted in English rather than fictional, social behaviour. I wanted to stress the naturalism of these scenes, by finding a context wherein Toby can be seen as the overgrown public schoolboy that he is, squandering his life in drink and practical jokes and Andrew as the lonely second son of a dwindling minor aristocratic family, devoid of qualifications and forlornly needing to make a money marriage to avert his impending bankruptcy.

They seem to me to exemplify a genre of truthful comedy, the comedy of recognition, and not at all to inhabit a grotesque or vaudeville world with which they have often been associated. Together with Maria (in this version, a governess of a certain age who sees her employment coming to an inevitable termination) they are at the centre of the third theme which is one of mortality, the passing of youth, the onset of age, the realization that happiness is brief and that time refuses to stand still. As Feste sings to the three of them, with the unerring pointed accuracy of an observer who sees through people: 'Youth's a stuff, 't will not endure'.

Mention of Feste returns me with a thump to the problems of textual length and esoteric language. It was urged to me more than once that Feste's speeches needed to be more heavily reduced, because often what he says is incomprehensible to the layman and I was told his songs hold up without contributing to the action.

Now given my chosen visual world of late nineteenth-century society, not altogether removed from Englishness, then Feste, as the traditional Elizabethan court jester, presented me with a major problem. But I had always believed that Feste was the central element of this many-faceted work who bound the contrasting ingredients together; Feste has a scene with every other protagonist and at some point, he shows them a view of themselves, a truth which often they would prefer to avoid, which requires his X-ray eyes to uncover. To reduce Feste to insignificance would be to torpedo the frail vessel and send it to the bottom.

My conclusion was that references to 'Fool' and 'Jester' shouldn't bother anybody, if I could make believable the kind of itinerant existence Feste leads and the narrative demands of his character. What do we know of him? He has long been absent, he knows that his future is threatened by Malvolio, he is often at Orsino's castle and not exclusively in the service of one employer, he was held in great affection by Olivia's father who died not so long ago, he is almost like a confessor to Olivia and yet a late-night drinking companion to Toby: he is Malvolio's natural enemy and he is a loner.

The image of a traveller, entirely uninterested in possessions, but with the reflexes of a beggar seemed to me to provide what Malvolio would revile, what Sir Toby would relate to, what Olivia would forgive, what Maria would scold, and that by which Viola would feel threatened, Sebastian pestered, and Orsino disturbed.

But at all events, as much as possible of the precious Feste cement had to stay if the building was to stand.

I thought it was in the *chronology* of the story that most change seemed to be necessary, requiring me to overcome my temerity about changing Shakespeare – after all, my dictat at the RSC had been 'we change him at our peril'.

Starting the story with the shipwrecked Viola on the shores of Illyria has often been done in stage productions. I realized for the film I wanted to go back one step further and start with Viola and Sebastian, before the shipwreck, happy and inseparable, partly to establish the 'twin' story as the main strand, partly for the audience to witness the loss of Sebastian, partly to introduce the distant adoration of Sebastian by Antonio and partly of course to have a movie opening of some elemental ferocity and emotional desperation.

It is clearly vital that an audience picks up that Viola, inconsolable about not just the loss of her brother but her *twin* brother, has no interest in going on living as herself; that is she feels instinctively that by *becoming* her twin brother she is in some sense preserving him. The more usual understanding, that a girl alone has to do something to protect herself, particularly in an alien country, would of course remain true.

I had always noted the several references to war in *Twelfth Night* but hadn't previously seen their importance. Orsino we learn has recently seen Antonio's face 'blackened by the smoke of war', Antonio knows he has 'many enemies at Orsino's court' and that he enjoys the status of fugitive, who will receive no mercy from those who he 'in terms so bloody and so dear' has made his enemies.

I thought the notion of establishing Illyria as 'enemy territory' for the shipwrecked survivors as well as for Antonio would provide a host of reasons for Viola's plight, her need for the Captain's help and the tension of her continuing fear of discovery. But to make this element of the story more coherent required the transposition of a few lines. The point I had reached was agonizing.

Twelfth Night was being prepared for the biggest audience who might so far have seen the work and yet here was I *tampering* with its perfect text. The constant reminder to myself that I was making a film – not filming a play – carried me to the point where, trembling and expecting an imminent thunderbolt, I wrote out the 'new' section.

I thought the credit sequence for the film (no stage production has to bother with *that* problem) should act as a division coming after what would be a prologue announcing the main ingredients of the plot and before the start of the work proper, which would still begin with one of the most famous opening lines in the canon: 'If music be the food of love, play on.'

Doing something once, Hamlet says to Gertrude, 'shall lend a kind of easiness to the next'. Thereafter the possibilities and necessities of a film structure for *Twelfth Night* cost me less sleep and became a source of much excitement. For example the biggest problem of the play in stage performance is that Orsino, who dominates the early part of the work, drops out at the end of Act Two and doesn't return again until the last scene of Act Five. In the film, I had a chance to alter the chronology so that the Viola/Orsino story could continue developing throughout, by being interleaved between Olivia scenes and Malvolio scenes, so that we never lose sight of the relationship about which we are required to be so joyously happy at the end.

Again, I was able to take the action to Olivia's house only when Viola first visits there on Orsino's behalf; that is, when she and therefore we are ready to meet a group of new characters. I could yoke together Orsino and Viola with Olivia, with Toby, Aguecheek and Maria all listening to the same evocative Feste music, thereby pulling the theme of the two plots into closer contact.

I could have Viola make her 'go-between' journey from Orsino to Olivia more times than actually happens in the play. Shakespeare gives us the *impression* that the journey happens several times, but when for the necessity of film definition, you count up the elapse of days and nights in the text, it's clear that the journey only happens twice and the whole story is in one sense over in just a day and a half. I say in one sense, because Shakespeare often employed a *double*-time scheme, speeding an audience along with one set of references suggesting a very short duration of the action, while in the same work (as in *Twelfth Night*) referring to an action lasting several months.

On film such essentially poetic contradictions or vaguaries work less well, because scenes are being photographed in a real climate, against real cloud scapes, during a real season, so it becomes much more necessary to be finite about the passage of time.

Given my new-found abandon, I was able to find ways of cutting text by creating shorter scenes in juxtaposition with each other, partly to achieve pace, but partly to accentuate meaning. For example, at the same time that Malvolio is protesting to Feste while locked up in the 'dark house' that he is not mad, Sebastian is arguing with himself about whether or not *he* is mad, or even whether Olivia is mad. When Feste gets Malvolio to say that he is as sane as anyone in Illyria, it is only a few seconds after Sebastian has shouted 'Are all the people mad?'

Film editing thrives on the energy and momentum of contrast and unlike on stage nobody has to enter or exit; the edit takes you to the next image instantly. So it was possible for me to divide the well-known 'ring' soliloquy into two sections, the first as Viola works out for herself what this gesture from Olivia really means; the second much later, in the depths of night, when Cesario, secretly able to become Viola again, is divesting herself of her disguise, which makes her think all over again about what it is to be a woman.

The liberating nature of film editing encouraged me to place Sebastian's reappearance within a whisker of Viola's route back to Orsino, so that not only, hopefully, does the audience momentarily confuse one twin with the other, but has the feeling that sooner or later the laws of coincidence will bring them together.

I say momentarily[1] because I think it is vital in this comedy that the audience are ahead of the confusions in the narrative. If, literally, the audience doesn't know which twin is Cesario and which Sebastian, then they are deprived of the laughter of watching other people getting wrong what they have got right. So I was never tempted by the (equally filmic) notion that twins can be played by the same actor. Indeed, with the help of technology, they can, but that technological ingredient always obtrudes and keeps the audience conscious that they are watching one actor's clever double performance and not two people.

No single performer in *Twelfth Night* can make the central proposition work, that these two people are identical but at the same time utterly different because of gender. So instead I searched for two performers who could look extremely alike when the plot demanded it, but whose differences were every bit as important as their similarities.

Film-making is finally about money, because time is money in the film business to a greater extent than in any other; a small budget means very little time to shoot in, and no time for rehearsal.

Now I cannot survive without rehearsal and so I managed to schedule just long enough to take each main character through their scenes once. In other words, I just had time to explain the text, the cuts, the background reasoning and to sit and analyse every word spoken, so that nobody would be uttering 'words, words, words' without the text becoming thought.

But I would have liked at least twice as long, even though I understand that 'spontaneity' can be threatened. When a scene is to be shot, the 'time' factor can become unbearable. The schedule

---

[1]This is English but no longer American for 'fleetingly – for but a moment'. In America, the word now means 'in a moment' or 'shortly'.

dictates everything and so an actor saying a wrong line is of little importance compared with the titanic problems of falling behind.Example: the crane camera and twenty horses are ordered for the afternoon, so whatever goes wrong in the morning the crane and the horses cannot be postponed, or the film must pay for them twice, or they aren't available again and a spiralling whirlwind of interlocking crises quickly develops.

But that insignificant misspoken piece of text that you didn't have time to go back on is in danger of being there for all time, a red rag to scholars and aficionados in a way which can never quite afflict a contemporary script wherein the text is not holy writ, or known in advance. I found myself fighting many an angry battle in defence of the text. It's a bit like a rugby match – you hug the opponents you have brutalized after the game.

When this film was first being set up, many internationally famous names were proposed as participants who would provide huge box-office value, despite, in most cases, never having played Shakespeare before. I tried to explain to the proposers the danger of this. I could collect, I said, a group of the world's greatest athletes, take them to a mountain top and put skis on their feet; only the ones who had been previously taught to ski would get down the mountain, and the others, however physically accomplished, would fall over, and the brave and determined ones might fall at speed and hurt themselves badly. Shakespeare doesn't respond to the belief that everything will be all right on the night, he has to be worked on and with, and worked at over time, before his locks begin to open.

In the end, despite the relatively small budget for the film (five million dollars, which by contemporary standards is just a bit more than a good television mini-series episode), I was overjoyed to have a cast who were skilled and comfortable in the idiom and who despite the privations of wind-swept Cornwall very late in the year, cared deeply about their work, about each other, and above all, about Shakespeare.

Together we made a film, an autumnal film, about the transience of youth, about the mysteries of sexuality, about hypocrisy and loneliness and facing the truth – with words by Shakespeare, but spoken to achieve the impression that none of them had ever been previously written down by a dramatist.

Film as I said is even more an amalgam of compromises than the theatre, and on more occasions than I care to remember I had to give up or give in to what I had determined not to. I had to lose yet further sections of the text in the editing process. Shakespeare's 'two hours traffic of the stage' has become Hollywood's holy writ – 'No film can work at the box-office if it is more than two hours long.'

And for my sins, I had to write a prologue, in blank verse, for Feste's voice, because those test-screening audiences still found the first section of the story difficult to comprehend. I invented an explanatory line (*mea culpa*, forgive me) to describe Orsino's all-male establishment, borrowed from *Love's Labours Lost*; I had to insert words to explain that this girl at the centre of things is called Viola, since Shakespeare omitted to mention her name other than in the cast list, until the last scene of the play. And finally I had to resist changing the title ... which as we say in the movies is where we came in.

*

As a direct result of the test-screening process, which took place in Orange County, California, I was asked to provide a form of voice-over introduction or explanation to ease the audience more comfortably into the story. It was clear they were taking time to get used to the heightened language, finding the verse and the vocabulary unfamiliar and therefore uncongenial. I concluded that, insofar as there was any such figure in *Twelfth Night* the story-teller character was Feste, and that it was not an impossibility that he should book-end the story by singing an opening stanza of 'The Rain it Raineth Every Day', the folk ballad with which he finishes the entertainment.

Having previously written lyrics culled from Shakespeare's text in a production of *The Comedy of Errors* and having contributed to two major musicals by writing the lyrics of 'Memory' in *Cats* and 'On My Own' in *Les Miserables* I nevertheless embarked on this task with a most pitiable temerity. The lyric I gave to Ben Kingsley eventually was very simple:

> I'll tell thee a tale, now list to me,
> With heigh ho, the wind and the rain.
> But merry or sad, which shall it be,
> For the rain it raineth every day.

This device provided the idea that a story of a fictional kind was going to be told, that it would include both comic and serious tones of voice and that the introductory circumstances could be fore-shortened in the 'once-upon-a-time' manner of myths and tall tales generally.

The message I was getting from the comprehension testing of preview audiences was that it was not clear that Viola and Sebastian were supposed to be brother and sister, or that she believed him to have drowned, or that there was any reason for her to feel threatened by arriving in Illyria. Above all there was the unanswered and in some ways unanswerable question 'Why does she decide to become a boy?'

Naturally I was disappointed by these results because I was

convinced that my wordless prologue had explained all these issues without the need for any accompanying pointers. But I agreed to experiment and myself recorded some lines I had written, having reread Shakespeare's earlier description of twins separated by shipwreck in the first scene of *The Comedy of Errors*. My text, still for Feste's voice, was probably, or should I say hopefully, full of unconscious borrowings, but was attempting to be pellucidly clear, which the Swan of Avon was never greatly fussed about. I thought I might try to solve the problem of the title while I was at it, with my tongue as much in my cheek as anybody needed it to be.

So, this concludes my confession; I resisted, I wept, I tampered. The love in the labour never diminished and the pleasure I took from being in Shakespeare's Illyria for a few months required no payment; which was lucky because in the end I had to contribute my fee to the completion of the film. I am left with only one problem, which is how, one of these days, to bring about the circumstances where I can do the play on stage without cutting or changing a word.

PROLOGUE

Once, upon Twelfth Night – or what you will –
Aboard a ship bound home to Messaline,
The festive company, dressed for masquerade
And singing songs each other to amuse
Delight above the rest in two young twins.

The storm has forc'd their vessel from its course
And now they strike upon submerged rocks.

Uncertain what to leave and what to save,
Brother and sister, orphaned since their father's death
Have but themselves alone in all the world.

The mighty billows tear one from the other.
Dauntless, her brother plunges in the main.

Deep currents and the sinking bark above them
Divide what naught had ever kept apart.

The poor survivors reach an alien shore
For Messaline with this country is at war.

TWELFTH NIGHT

CAST *in order of speaking*

VIOLA	Imogen Stubbs
CAPTAIN	Sid Livingstone
ORSINO	Toby Stephens
VALENTINE	Alan Mitchell
MARIA	Imelda Staunton
SIR TOBY BELCH	Mel Smith
SIR ANDREW AGUECHEEK	Richard E. Grant
FESTE	Ben Kingsley
MALVOLIO	Nigel Hawthorne
OLIVIA	Helena Bonham Carter
ANTONIO	Nicholas Farrell
SEBASTIAN	Stephen Mackintosh
FABIAN	Peter Gunn
FIRST OFFICER	Timothy Bentinck
SECOND OFFICER	Rod Culbertson
PRIEST	James Walker
Director	Trevor Nunn
Producers	Stephen Evans and David Parfitt
Executive Producer	Greg Smith
Screenplay	Trevor Nunn
Director of Photography	Clive Tickner
Production Designer	Sophie Becher
Editor	Peter Boyle
Costume Designer	John Bright
Make-up Designer	Christine Beveridge
Music	Shaun Davey

1. EXT. NIGHT. SEA.
The sea, surging and angry, ceaselessly rolling, mounting and crashing, is almost obscured by slanting rain.

2. INT. NIGHT. SHIP.
A steamer, big enough to carry fifty passengers, with some cabins and deck areas, lurches through the spray.

3. INT. NIGHT. SHIP.
Some thirty or so passengers are sitting in a saloon, thick with smoke, being entertained by two girls, one at a piano, the other with a concertina, singing a music hall song that has the audience convulsed. The song is called 'O mistress mine'. As the girls arrive at the line: 'That can sing both high and low', one voice is indeed soprano but the other is baritone. They turn and look at each other. They are both wearing 'yashmaks' covering their mouths and they look identical. They sing again, and again the voices separate into male and female. The audience laughs again.

The girl with the concertina reaches forward and pulls down the 'yashmak' of the girl at the piano – revealing a small moustache. The audience laughter increases. The girl at the piano reaches out and pulls the yashmak from the other girl – also revealing a small moustache.

ANTONIO, *a forty-year-old man dressed in military uniform, sits at a table drinking and watches intently, not sharing the laughter around him, but concentrating on the concertina player.*

3

The concertina girl leans across and deftly placing finger and thumb on the end of the piano girl's moustache, peels it away. The piano girl, fully confirmed as a girl, now reaches up to the concertina girl's moustache. Suddenly the ship lurches and the piano rolls several feet away, separating the two performers.

4. EXT. NIGHT. SHIP.
The steamer plunges almost perpendicularly down a massive wave and smashes through the next one almost disappearing under the spray and wash.

5. INT. NIGHT. SHIP.
The musical twins sense the alarm in the audience as the ship lurches again and the piano rolls in the opposite direction, crashing into a table and scattering the revellers.

6. INT. NIGHT. SHIP.
ANTONIO stands up and moves to a porthole as other passengers watch him. He turns back in alarm. The 'girl' with the concertina slowly pulls a wig off, revealing himself to be an eighteen-year-old boy. He is SEBASTIAN, the twin brother of the girl at the piano, who is VIOLA. A WOMAN screams and pandemonium is unleashed.

7. INT. NIGHT. SHIP.
The storm has worsened and the steamer is bucketing and lurching out of control.

8. EXT. NIGHT. SHIP.
SEBASTIAN and VIOLA are packing their things into a trunk. He divests himself of his costume and pulls out two uniforms, trying to find which one is his. She picks up a photograph of the

5

two of them at a piano with an older man, their father. She looks at her brother. He takes the photograph, as a massive rending noise precedes crashes and shudders above them.

9. EXT. NIGHT. SHIP.
Amongst a panic of other passengers, VIOLA *is coming up on deck helped by* SEBASTIAN, *now dressed as a naval cadet in a dark uniform, which he is trying to button up. They are thrown off balance and drenched in spray as sailors plunge through the crowd shouting whilst some others struggle with winching down a lifeboat.* ANTONIO *grabs the twins but loses his grip on* VIOLA, *who is swept overboard.* SEBASTIAN *screams and leaps in to the sea to save* VIOLA.

10. EXT. NIGHT. UNDER THE SEA.
VIOLA *sinks down in slow motion, her skirts clinging and ballooning.* VIOLA *sees* SEBASTIAN *tumbling spread-eagled in the slow-motion water. They reach out for each other, like embryos in a womb.*

11. EXT. NIGHT. SEA.
For a few seconds as they surface, VIOLA *sees* SEBASTIAN *as a* SAILOR *grabs her and tries to help her.* SEBASTIAN *is swept away and* VIOLA *breaks free of the* SAILOR, *trying to swim after her brother. She flounders.*

12. EXT. NIGHT. SHIP'S DECK.
ANTONIO *climbs up on to the ship's rail, scouring the waves for a sight of* SEBASTIAN.

13. EXT. NIGHT. SEA.

VIOLA *struggles hysterically as she is held up by the* SAILOR
(CAPTAIN). *Her brother is no longer visible.*

14. EXT. NIGHT. BEACH.

VIOLA *and some sailors are struggling through the waves to the
shore.*

15. EXT. DAWN. BEACH.

*The sea is calmer – as wreckage and possessions float
pathetically towards the shore.* VIOLA *is shaking in shock,
sitting on the sand, surrounded by prone and exhausted sailors.*

VIOLA:
  What country, friends, is this?
CAPTAIN:
  This is Illyria, lady.
VIOLA:
  And what should I do in Illyria?
  My brother, he is in Elysium.
  VIOLA *sobs uncontrollably.*

16. EXT. DAY. BEACH.

The sun is coming up. The twins' trunk is washed ashore.
VIOLA *opens the box and pulls out clothing, including her
'cadet' costume matching with* SEBASTIAN's.

VIOLA:
  Perchance he is not drowned.
CAPTAIN: My lady Viola,
  It is perchance that you yourself were saved.
VIOLA:
  O, my poor brother!

The CAPTAIN *restrains her as she starts to run in despair back into the sea.*

17. EXT. DAY. BEACH.
Some soldiers on horseback are distantly visible coming towards the huddled group. The CAPTAIN *urges his sailors and* VIOLA *to hide in a cave nearby.*

18. EXT. DAY. BEACH.
The soldiers ride up, circling and prodding the flotsam and jetsam in a brutal cursory way, and then ride off.

19. EXT. DAY. CAVE.
The sailors and VIOLA *crouch in hiding.* VIOLA *is trembling with fear and cold.*

VIOLA:
   Knowest thou this country?
CAPTAIN (*grimly*):
   Ay, madam, well,
   Two sailors keep watch at the mouth of the cave as the
   CAPTAIN *responds to* VIOLA's *questioning look.*
CAPTAIN:
   The quarrel between the merchants here and ours
   Too oft has given us bloody argument.
   We must not be discovered in this place.
   A low whistle catches the attention of the whispering group.
   One of the sailors at the mouth of the cave beckons them now
   that all is clear. They move off towards the beach.

8

20. EXT. DAY. CLIFFTOP.
An unshaven unkempt man – part vagabond, part itinerant entertainer – is huddled on the cliffs way above the desolate survivors. He stares down at them. The man is FESTE.

21. EXT. DAY. BEACH.
VIOLA *takes off a necklace, throws it in the sand, and stands staring at the sea, holding the cadet uniform from the trunk.*
    The group with bundles and oddments rescued from the wreckage move along the beach below the cliff wall.

22. EXT. DAY. ROAD.
As a farm wagon clops away from them along a deserted road, the fugitive group scurry out of a ditch across the road and into the bushes beyond.

23. EXT. DAY. WOODS.
The group is resting up in a clearing in the trees, sitting, squatting and eating. Two of the sailors stare at VIOLA. *She becomes uncomfortably self-conscious, realizing she is a girl alone amongst men.*

VIOLA:
  Who governs here?
CAPTAIN:
  The Duke Orsino.
VIOLA:
  Orsino ... I have heard my father name him.
  He was a bachelor then.
CAPTAIN:
  And so is now, or was so, very late;
  For but a month ago 'twas fresh in murmur
  That he did seek the love of fair Olivia.

He stops and listens intently. They hear the approach of horses and see a group of soldiers ride distantly into view. In some panic the group go deeper into the wood and tumble over a wall. Just as they think they are safe, they hear a bell tolling close by and plangent organ music. They all hide amongst the trees.

24. EXT. DAY. OLIVIA'S ESTATE. CHURCHYARD.
A family group is leaving a graveside and walking in procession past a small church towards a mansion. A young woman (OLIVIA), *her face visible through a veil, is being supported by a grimly serious older man* (MALVOLIO), *followed by a heavily veiled old lady and a frock-coated gentleman walking infirmly with a stick. A corpulent and uncomfortable middle-aged man* (SIR TOBY BELCH) *comes next, followed by a woman of a certain age who would be taken for a governess* (MARIA), *and some members of the household, all dressed uniformly in black.*

25. EXT. DAY. OLIVIA'S ESTATE. WALL AND TREES.

VIOLA:
  What's she?
CAPTAIN:
  That same Olivia, the daughter of a count
  That died some twelvemonth since; her brother,
  Has lately also died; for whose dear love,
  They say, she hath abjured the sight
  And company of men.
  VIOLA *fights back her tears recognizing that* OLIVIA's *situation is her own.*
    The procession disappears towards the house.
VIOLA:
  O, that I served that lady,

11

And might not be delivered to the world –
Till I had made mine own occasion mellow –
What my estate is.

CAPTAIN: That were hard to compass,
Because she will admit no kind of suit,
No, not the Duke's.

VIOLA grabs the bundle of clothes she has been carrying and unfolds the uniform.

VIOLA: I prithee be my aid
For such disguise as haply shall become
The form of my intent. I'll serve this Duke.

The CAPTAIN shakes his head and begins to walk away.
VIOLA follows him.

VIOLA:
I shall present me as a boy to him.
It may be worth thy pains, for I can sing
And speak to him in many sorts of music
That will allow me very worth his service.

The CAPTAIN shrugs and smiles.

VIOLA:
I thank thee.

26. INT. DAY.

MONTAGE/CREDIT SEQUENCE
The credits (as few front credits as possible) are laid over a sequence of VIOLA being transformed into a boy (CESARIO); cutting her hair; binding her chest; putting on trousers and braces; realizing the crutch needs padding; experimenting with a rolled handkerchief; trying to button her shirt the wrong way; growling and hurting her voice to lower it; trying out different walks; whistling; fully clothed looking unconvinced in a mirror; taking out a photograph of her and her brother; taking out the pieces of a small blond moustache.

27. EXT. DAY. ORSINO'S CASTLE.

A young man walks across a causeway towards an austere castle dramatically perched on a rocky island, surrounded by crashing waves.

28. INT. DAY. ORSINO'S CASTLE. DRAWING-ROOM.

Portraits glisten in the curtained half-light. A group of military gentlemen wait patiently in various stages of boredom and frustration as an ornate piece of piano music reaches its conclusion. The impression is of a military academy. A young militarily-dressed man lies full-length on a chaise, his left hand covering his eyes, his right arm cradled in a sling, as if recovering from a battle wound. This is ORSINO.

ORSINO:
    If music be the food of love, play on,
    Give me excess of it, that, surfeiting,
    The appetite may sicken, and so die.
    The piano plays on to a further movement.
ORSINO:
    That strain again!
    For the first time, we see the pianist. It is VIOLA, *dressed completely to look identical to the last time we saw* SEBASTIAN *and wearing the moustache that she had been contemplating.* VIOLA *has called herself '*CESARIO*'.* ORSINO*'s command bewilders* CESARIO, *but a grey-haired servant,* CURIO, *nods that she is to repeat the last section.*

29. EXT. DAY. ORSINO'S CASTLE. STEPS.

An elderly servant climbs the steps which wind steeply upwards from the distant sea below, and wearily enters the house.

13

30. INT. DAY. ORSINO'S CASTLE. DRAWING-ROOM.

ORSINO: It had a dying fall.
  O, it came o'er my ear like the sweet sound
  That breathes upon a bank of violets,
  Stealing and giving odour. Enough, no more!
  ORSINO suddenly gets up and walks over to the piano,
  closing the lid. CESARIO *is shocked.* ORSINO *is*
  apologetic.

ORSINO:
  'Tis not so sweet now as it was before.
  He goes to lean against a massive stone archway.

ORSINO:
  O spirit of love, how quick and fresh art thou,
  That, notwithstanding thy capacity
  Receiveth as the sea, naught enters there,
  Of what validity and pitch soe'er,
  But falls into abatement and low price
  Even in a minute. So full of shapes is fancy
  That it alone is high fantastical.
  The elderly servant, VALENTINE, *arrives at the end of his*
  long journey.

ORSINO:
  How now! What news from her?

VALENTINE (*fighting for breath*):
  So please my lord, I might not be admitted,
  But from her handmaid do return this answer:
  He takes a paper from his inside coat pocket and reads.

VALENTINE:
  The element itself, till seven years' heat,
  Shall not behold her face at ample view,
  But like a cloistress –
  ORSINO snatches it away and reads it himself.

ORSINO: – all this to season
  A brother's dead love, which she would keep fresh

14

And lasting, in her sad remembrance.

ORSINO turns unsteadily and fighting his distress, speaks unexpectedly. to CESARIO.

ORSINO:

O, she that hath a heart of that fine frame
To pay this debt of love but to a brother –

His words inadvertently strike a vulnerable chord in CESARIO and briefly we catch a glimpse of the image of SEBASTIAN drowning. ORSINO goes urgently out of the room followed in despairing frustration by his military attendants who once again have failed to get their commander to concentrate on their needs.

31. INT. DAY. ORSINO'S HOUSE. GYMNASIUM.

A FENCING MASTER is taking class at ORSINO's fencing school. CESARIO is practising lunging at a partner. The FENCING MASTER holds CESARIO around the waist and adjusts her lunging posture. His hands touch the hips and padded chest of his pupil, who is secretly very alarmed. CESARIO suddenly stiffens as she sees ORSINO enter at the far end, his arm now only bandaged.

CESARIO: Here comes the Count.

ORSINO: Who saw Cesario, ha?

CESARIO takes off her mask.

CESARIO: On your attendance, my lord, here.

He strides up to his new favourite.

ORSINO: Cesario?

He motions that they should leave but CESARIO is painfully aware of masked stares. ORSINO's arm goes round CESARIO's shoulder as they walk away.

32. EXT. DAY. ORSINO'S CASTLE. ROCKS AND SHORE.

ORSINO *leads a nervous* CESARIO *across the rocks below the castle to the shore line.*

ORSINO *is sitting by the sea, with the castle in the background, next to* CESARIO, *having told the whole story of his love for* OLIVIA.

ORSINO:
Thou knowest no less but all. I have unclasped
To thee the book even of my secret soul.
Therefore, good youth, address thy gait unto her.
CESARIO *is uncomfortably surprised.*

ORSINO:
Be not denied access; stand at her doors,
And tell them, there thy fixed foot shall grow
Till thou have audience.
Clearly, CESARIO *doesn't want the job.*

CESARIO: Sure, my noble lord,
If she be so abandoned to her sorrow
As it is spake, she never will admit me.

ORSINO:
Be clamorous and leap all civil bounds.

CESARIO:
Say I do speak with her, my lord, what then?

ORSINO:
O, then unfold the passion of my love.
It shall become thee well to act my woes;
She will attend it better in thy youth.

CESARIO:
I think not so, my lord.

ORSINO: Dear lad, believe it
For they shall yet belie thy happy years
That say thou art a man.
ORSINO *pushes* CESARIO *down and leans over the 'boy' who wrestles in involuntary alarm.*

16

ORSINO: Diana's lip
   Is not more smooth and rubious. Thy small pipe
   Is as the maiden's organ, shrill and sound,
   And all is semblative a woman's part.
   CESARIO *pushes* ORSINO *away.* ORSINO *laughs for the*
   first time, but in the horseplay, he thumps his wounded arm
   on a rock.

33. EXT. DAY. ORSINO'S CASTLE. DRAWING-ROOM.
CESARIO, *still dressed in uniform with a sword, is receiving*
final instructions from a pale ORSINO *lying on the couch with a*
rug pulled over him.

ORSINO:
   I know thy constellation is right apt
   For this affair. Some four or five attend him.
   CESARIO *sets off on the journey to* OLIVIA, *accompanied by*
   a few other servants, pausing to look once more in concern at
   ORSINO.

34. EXT. DAY. CAUSEWAY.
The small group is walking, listlessly towards the mainland.

35. EXT. DAY. THE CLIFFS BETWEEN ORSINO'S CASTLE AND
OLIVIA'S HOUSE.
The cadets stroll unhurriedly with CESARIO *along the cliff*
path.

36. EXT. DAY. OLIVIA'S HOUSE. DAIRY, CORRIDOR AND
KITCHEN/SCULLERY.
The butler, MALVOLIO, *is doing his early morning rounds. He*
surveys the work in the dairy, as the women stop and curtsey to
him. In a kind of royal progress, he strides, followed by two

17

junior men of his staff and MARIA, *past the bakery room and into the kitchen which he circles, bringing all the work of the kitchen staff to a respectful halt. As he is inspecting the preparations of the day's food,* MARIA *has her attention caught, by* FABIAN, *an under-gardner, who is standing uneasily amongst the women in the scullery. He makes sign language of a problem to her, and she slips off, anxiously watching that* MALVOLIO *does not notice her.*

37. EXT. DAY. OLIVIA'S HOUSE. GARDEN.
MARIA *and* FABIAN *pass through a formal garden to some steps leading down to a sunken garden where* SIR TOBY *is asleep, still fully dressed in the clothes of last night's binge and still clutching a wine bottle.*

MARIA: By my troth, Sir Toby, you must come in earlier o'nights. Your cousin, my lady, takes great exceptions to your ill hours.
SIR TOBY: Why, let her except before excepted.
   FABIAN *and* MARIA *help* SIR TOBY *up.*
      Largely supported by FABIAN, SIR TOBY *crosses the garden to the hallway with* MARIA.

38. INT. DAY. OLIVIA'S HOUSE. HALLWAY.

MARIA: That quaffing and drinking will undo you. I heard my lady talk of it yesterday –
   She indicates for FABIAN *to leave them.*
MARIA: – and of a foolish knight that you brought in one night here, to be her wooer.
SIR TOBY: Who? Sir Andrew Aguecheek?
MARIA: Ay, he.
SIR TOBY: He's as tall a man as any's in Illyria.
MARIA: What's that to the purpose?
   18

SIR TOBY: Why, he has three thousand ducats a year. He speaks three or four languages word for word without book.

MARIA: He's a fool, he's a great quarreller; and but that he hath the gift of a coward, 'tis thought he would quickly have the gift of a grave.

39. INT. DAY. OLIVIA'S HOUSE. STAIRS/HALL.

SIR ANDREW AGUECHEEK *appears looking down from an upper landing.*

SIR ANDREW: Sir Toby Belch!

SIR TOBY: Sir Andrew Agueface!

SIR ANDREW: How now, Sir Toby Belch?

SIR TOBY: Sweet Sir Andrew!

They meet in the hallway, but the noise of their talk attracts the attention of chambermaids who watch from various places.

SIR ANDREW: Bless you, fair shrew.

MARIA: And you too, sir.

SIR TOBY: Accost, Sir Andrew, accost.

SIR ANDREW: What's that?

SIR TOBY: My niece's chambermaid.

SIR ANDREW: Good Mistress Accost, I desire better acquaintance.

MARIA: My name is Mary, sir.

SIR ANDREW: Good Mistress Mary Accost –

There is giggling and murmuring from the chambermaids above.

SIR TOBY (*aside*): 'Accost' is front her, board her, woo her, assail her.

SIR ANDREW (*aside*): By my troth, I would not undertake her in this company.

MARIA: Fare you well, gentlemen.

SIR ANDREW: Is that the meaning of 'accost'?

MARIA *leaves for her office, whispering to a young manservant as she goes.* SIR TOBY *sighs at* SIR ANDREW'*s gauche incomprehension.*

40. INT. DAY. OLIVIA'S HOUSE. BALLROOM.

SIR TOBY *walks into the ballroom which has curtained windows letting in only slivers of light.* SIR ANDREW *follows disconsolately.* SIR TOBY *begins to tug at the curtains letting more and more light stream into the darkened room.*

SIR TOBY: What a plague means my niece to take the death of her brother thus! I am sure care's an enemy to life.

SIR ANDREW: I'll ride home tomorrow, Sir Toby.

SIR TOBY (*with some attempt to cover his disquiet*): *Pourquoi,* my dear knight?

SIR ANDREW: What is *pourquoi?* Do or not do? I would I had bestowed that time in the tongues that I have in fencing and dancing. O, had I but followed the arts!

SIR TOBY *is brought tea and raw eggs by the manservant who was previously instructed by* MARIA. SIR TOBY *swallows his 'medicine'.*

SIR ANDREW: Faith, I'll home tomorrow, Sir Toby. Your niece will not be seen, or if she be, it's four to one she'll none of me; the Count himself, here hard by, woos her.

The manservant leaves down the length of the ballroom.

SIR TOBY: She'll none o'the Count, she'll not match above her degree. I have heard her swear't. Tut, there's life in't, man.

SIR ANDREW: I'll stay a month longer. I am a fellow o'the strangest mind i'the world. I delight in masques and revels sometimes altogether.

SIR TOBY: Art thou good at these kickshawses, knight?

SIR ANDREW: Faith, I can cut a caper. And I think I have
the back-trick, simply as strong as any man in Illyria.
SIR TOBY *sits and bangs out a tune on the grand piano as*
SIR ANDREW *waltzes.*

SIR TOBY: Wherefore are these things hid? Wherefore have
these gifts a curtain before 'em?
SIR TOBY *changes his piano accompaniment to throw* SIR
ANDREW *into different dance steps.*

SIR TOBY: Why dost thou not go to church in a galliard and
come home in a coranto? Is it a world to hide virtues in?

SIR ANDREW: Shall we set about some revels?

SIR TOBY: What shall we do else? Let me see thee caper.
Ha! Higher! Ha! Ha! Excellent!
The steward, MALVOLIO, *appears at the end of the long*
room. SIR TOBY *sees him and instantly, under* MALVOLIO's
displeased stare, the music stops. SIR ANDREW *looks*
stricken, as he must have done as a child.

41. INT. DAY. OLIVIA'S HOUSE. THE STUDY/LIBRARY.
MARIA *is sitting working at the household books, copying bills,*
and writing from OLIVIA's *handwritten notes. She looks up*
and sees FESTE *signalling to her outside.*

42. EXT. DAY. OLIVIA'S HOUSE. CORRIDOR AND KITCHEN.
MARIA *is remonstrating with* FESTE *in a corridor, then taking*
him round to the kitchen.

MARIA: Nay, either tell me where thou has been, or I will
not open my lips so wide as a bristle may enter, in way of
thy excuse. My lady will hang thee for thy absence.

FESTE: Let her hang me. I fear no colours.

MARIA: I can tell thee where that saying was born.

FESTE: Where, good Mistress Mary?

MARIA: In the war.

22

FESTE: Well, God give them wisdom that have it; and those that are fools, let them use their talents.

MARIA *gets him some bread and beer, watched by several other maids and the cook whose disapproval is clear.*

MARIA: You are resolute, then?

FESTE: I am resolved on two points.

MARIA: That if one break, the other will hold; or if both break, your breeches fall.

MARIA *is about to leave.*

FESTE: Well, go thy way, if Sir Toby would leave drinking, thou wert as witty a piece of Eve's flesh as any in Illyria.

FESTE *has obviously hit on a sensitive subject and* MARIA *rounds on him.*

MARIA: Peace, you rogue, no more o'that.

43. INT. DAY. CHURCH NEAR OLIVIA'S HOUSE.

A tearful OLIVIA *is leaving church with* MARIA. MALVOLIO *kneels in his pew at his prayers for longer than everybody else. He gets up as they pass. The* PRIEST *stands in the porch as the congregation trickles out.*

44. EXT. DAY. PATH FROM CHURCH TO OLIVIA'S HOUSE.

FESTE *steps out into* OLIVIA'*s path. She is obviously displeased that he is there.*

FESTE: God bless thee, lady!

OLIVIA: Take the fool away.

FESTE: Do you not hear, fellows? Take away the lady.

OLIVIA: Go to. I'll no more of you. Besides, you grow dishonest.

OLIVIA *walks on towards the house with her small entourage – * FESTE *stays with them and continues to badger her, thereby creating obvious tension.*

FESTE: Bid the dishonest man mend himself: if he mend, he is no longer dishonest; if he cannot, let the botcher mend him. Anything that's mended, is but patched; virtue that transgresses is but patched with sin; and sin that amends is but patched with virtue. As there is no true cuckold but calamity, so beauty's a flower. The lady bade take away the fool; therefore I say again – take her away!

OLIVIA: Sir, I bade them take away you.

FESTE: Misprision, in the highest degree! Good madonna, give me leave to prove you a fool.

OLIVIA *stops on the path in view of the gatehouse.*

OLIVIA: Can you do it?

FESTE: Dexteriously, good madonna.

OLIVIA: Make your proof.

FESTE: I must catechize you for it, madonna. Good my mouse of virtue, answer me.

OLIVIA: Well, sir, for want of other idleness.

FESTE: Good madonna, why mourn'st thou?

OLIVIA (*sensitive to this apparently insensitive question*): Good fool, for my brother's death.

FESTE: I think his soul is in hell, madonna.

OLIVIA (*stung*): I know his soul is in heaven, fool.

FESTE: The more fool, madonna, to mourn for your brother's soul, being in heaven. Take away the fool, gentlemen.

OLIVIA (*in spite of herself, seeing* FESTE's *good intention*): What think you of this fool, Malvolio? Doth he not mend?

MALVOLIO: Yes, and shall do, till the pangs of death shake him. Infirmity, that decays the wise, doth ever make the better fool.

FESTE *is shocked by this venomous attack.*

FESTE: God send you, sir, a speedy infirmity for the better increasing your folly.

OLIVIA: How say you to that, Malvolio?

MALVOLIO: I marvel your ladyship takes delight in such a barren rascal. Look you now, he's out of his guard already; unless you laugh and minister occasion to him, he is gagged.

OLIVIA (*whispering*): O, you are sick of self-love, Malvolio, and taste with a distempered appetite.

OLIVIA *goes to embrace* FESTE – *a welcome home clasp*.

OLIVIA: There is no slander in an allowed fool, though he do nothing but rail; nor no railing in a known discreet man, though he do nothing but reprove.

FESTE *and* MALVOLIO *glare implacably at each other as* MARIA – *having been approached by another servant – explains a problem*.

MARIA: Madam, there is at the gate a young gentleman much desires to speak with you.

OLIVIA (*suddenly behaving like a panicked teenager*): From the Count Orsino, is it?

MARIA: I know not, madam.

OLIVIA: Who of my people hold him in delay?

MARIA (*reluctant and embarrassed*): Sir Toby, madam.

OLIVIA: He speaks nothing but madman. Go you, Malvolio. If it be a suit from the Count, I am sick or not at home – what you will, to dismiss it.

OLIVIA *goes into the house, turning to beckon to* FESTE *without* MALVOLIO *seeing her*.

45. INT. DAY. OLIVIA'S HOUSE. DRAWING-ROOM.

OLIVIA *goes up to the massive mirror and removes her hat*.

OLIVIA: Now you see, sir, how your fooling grows old and people dislike it?

OLIVIA *faces* FESTE, *realizes how much she has missed him during this terrible time of grief and goes to him for comfort. He cradles her, as he did when she was much younger.*

FESTE: Thou hast spoke for us, madonna, as if thy eldest son should be a fool; whose skull Jove cram with brains, for – here he comes – one of thy kin has a most weak *pia mater.*

SIR TOBY *comes in, knocking a flower arrangement over, followed by* MARIA, *who is caught between excusing* SIR TOBY *and being stern on* OLIVIA's *behalf.*

OLIVIA: By mine honour, half drunk! What is he at the gate, cousin?

SIR TOBY: A gentleman.

OLIVIA: A gentleman! What gentleman?

SIR TOBY: 'Tis a gentleman here ... (*He burps involuntarily.*) – a plague o'these pickle-herring! How now, sot!

SIR TOBY *hugs* FESTE *in a hugely unsteady gesture.*

FESTE: Good Sir Toby!

OLIVIA: Cousin, cousin, how have you come so early by this lethargy?

SIR TOBY: Lechery! I defy lechery! There's one at the gate.

OLIVIA: Ay, marry, what is he?

SIR TOBY: Let him be the devil an he will, I care not. Give me faith, say I. Well, it's all one.

SIR TOBY *goes out and upstairs as much like a bishop as he can manage.*

OLIVIA: What's a drunken man like?

FESTE: Like a drowned man, a fool, and a madman. One draught above heat makes him a fool, the second mads him, and a third drowns him.

OLIVIA: Go thou and seek the coroner ... (*Indicating* SIR TOBY.) He's drowned.

FESTE: He is but mad yet, madonna.

FESTE *goes out and upstairs in search of* SIR TOBY.

46. EXT. DAY. OLIVIA'S HOUSE. TERRACE.

MALVOLIO *appears outside the French windows. He enters from the garden.*

47. INT. DAY. OLIVIA'S HOUSE. DRAWING-ROOM.

OLIVIA *lies down on sofa.*

MALVOLIO: Madam, yond young fellow swears he will speak with you. I told him you were sick; I told him you were asleep –

OLIVIA (*with some irritation*): Tell him, he shall not speak with me.

MALVOLIO: Has been told so; and he says he'll stand at your door like a sheriff's post but he'll speak with you.

OLIVIA (*with the beginnings of interest*): What kind o'man is he?

MALVOLIO: Why, of mankind.

OLIVIA: What manner of man?

MALVOLIO: Of very ill manner; he'll speak with you, will you or no.

OLIVIA: Of what personage and years is he?

MALVOLIO: Not yet old enough for a man, nor young enough for a boy; as a squash is before 'tis a peascod. One would think his mother's milk were scarce out of him.

OLIVIA: Let him approach. Call in my gentlewoman.

MALVOLIO *is displeased that the young pipsqueak he is describing seems to have prevailed. He goes dyspeptically to the stairs.*

MALVOLIO: Gentlewoman, my lady calls.

MARIA *comes hurrying down.* MALVOLIO *makes clear his disapproval of her time spent with* SIR TOBY, *before leaving once again for the front gate.*

OLIVIA:
Give me my veil. Come, throw it o'er my face.
We'll once more hear Orsino's embassy.

MARIA *knows the routine of the veil; she lights some candles and closes the curtains, as two other women servants sit in the room, in a flurry, followed by stillness. Footsteps. There is a tap on the door. The door opens.* CESARIO *nervously peers in.*

CESARIO (*whispering into the gloom*): The honourable lady of the house, which is she?

OLIVIA: Speak to me, I shall answer for her. Your will?

CESARIO *approaches* OLIVIA.

CESARIO: Most radiant, exquisite, and unmatched beauty – *She notices one servant girl almost laughing catching the eye of another – the breeze twitching the curtain showing the window is open.*

CESARIO: I pray you, tell me if this be the lady of the house, for I never saw her. I would be loath to cast away my speech. I have taken great pains to learn it.

OLIVIA: Whence came you, sir?

CESARIO: That question's out of my part. Good gentle one, give me modest assurance if you be the lady of the house.

OLIVIA: Are you a comedian?

CESARIO: No, my profound heart. Are you the lady of the house?

OLIVIA: I am.

CESARIO *begins to find some bravado in the face of this perverse situation.*

CESARIO: Then I will on with my speech in your praise.

OLIVIA: Come to what is important in't. I forgive you the praise.

CESARIO: Alas, I took great pains to study it, and 'tis poetical.

OLIVIA: It is the more like to be feigned. I heard you were saucy at my gates, and allowed your approach rather to wonder at you than to hear you. If you be mad, be gone; if you have reason, be brief.

MARIA *stands up and goes to* CESARIO.

MARIA: Will you hoist sail, sir? Here lies your way.

MARIA *takes* CESARIO *quite forcibly by the arm.*

CESARIO: No, good swabber, I am to hull here a little longer. Some mollification for your giant, sweet lady!

OLIVIA (*resignedly*): Speak your office.

CESARIO: It alone concerns your ear. I bring no overture of war, my words are as full of peace as matter.

OLIVIA: Yet you began rudely. What are you? What would you?

CESARIO: The rudeness that hath appeared in me have I learned from my entertainment. What I am and what I would are as secret as maidenhead; to your ears divinity, to any others profanation.

OLIVIA: Give us the place alone.

MARIA, *in some amazement, and the servants leave; there is the faintest laughter in the corridor.*

OLIVIA: We will hear this divinity.

She moves to a chair close to some candles and a bible rest.

OLIVIA: Now, sir, what is your text?

CESARIO: Most sweet lady —

OLIVIA: A comfortable doctrine, and much may be said of it. Where lies your text?

CESARIO: In Orsino's bosom.

OLIVIA: In his bosom! In what chapter of his bosom?

CESARIO: In the first of his heart.

OLIVIA: O, I have read it; it is heresy. Have you no more to say?

OLIVIA *sits in the protection of the darkest corner of the room.*

CESARIO: Good madam, let me see your face.

OLIVIA: Have you any commission from your lord to negotiate with my face? You are now out of your text; but we will draw the curtain and show you the picture.

She takes off her veil and is faintly lit by the candles.

OLIVIA: Look you, sir, such a one I was this present. Is't not well done?

CESARIO: Excellently done – if God did all.

OLIVIA: 'Tis in grain, sir, 'twill endure wind and weather.

CESARIO suddenly pulls open the window curtain nearby – OLIVIA squints, but recovers her composure as the daylight floods in. CESARIO sees OLIVIA properly for the first time.

CESARIO:
'Tis beauty truly blent.
Lady, you are the cruellest she alive,
If you will lead these graces to the grave,
And leave the world no copy.

OLIVIA: O, sir, I will not be so hard-hearted. I will give out divers schedules of my beauty.

She gets up confidently and moves about the room.

OLIVIA: It shall be inventoried, and every particle and utensil labelled as, item: two lips, indifferent red; item: two eyes, with lids to them; item: one neck, one chin, and so forth.

CESARIO confronts her.

CESARIO:
I see you what you are, you are too proud.
But if you were the devil, you are fair.
My lord and master loves you – O, such love
Could be but recompensed, though you were crowned
The nonpareil of beauty!

OLIVIA: How does he love me?

CESARIO:
With adorations, fertile tears,
With groans that thunder love, with sighs of fire.

The impact of this close-up declaration has a destabilizing effect on OLIVIA.

OLIVIA:
Your lord does know my mind, I cannot love him.

OLIVIA *steps outside to the terrace, needing to distance herself from such a passionate advance.*

48. EXT. DAY. OLIVIA'S HOUSE. TERRACE AND GARDEN.
CESARIO *follows her to the window, steps out to the terrace and then out into the garden.*

OLIVIA:
   Yet I suppose him virtuous, know him noble,
   Of great estate, of fresh and stainless youth,
   Learned and valiant. But yet I cannot love him.
   He might have took his answer long ago.
CESARIO:
   If I did love you in my master's flame,
   With such a suffering, such a deadly life,
   In your denial I would find no sense;
   I would not understand it.
OLIVIA: Why, what would you?
CESARIO:
   Make me a willow cabin at your gate,
   And call upon my soul within the house;
   Write loyal cantons of contemnèd love
   And sing them loud even in the dead of night;
   (*Yelling out.*)
   Halloo your name to the reverberate hills
   And make the babbling gossip of the air
   Cry out 'Olivia!'

49. INT. DAY. OLIVIA'S HOUSE. CORRIDOR.
MALVOLIO *reacts anxiously at this yell and sets off to investigate.*

50. EXT. DAY. OLIVIA'S HOUSE. THE GARDEN.

CESARIO: O, you should not rest
  Between the elements of air and earth,
  But you should pity me.
  Again, OLIVIA*'s defences are shaken.*
OLIVIA: You might do much.
  What is your parentage?
CESARIO:
  Above my fortunes, yet my state is well.
  I am a gentleman.
  OLIVIA *walks towards the gate, troubled and distracted.*
OLIVIA: Get you to your lord.
  I cannot love him. Let him send no more –
  She opens the gate and CESARIO *steps through.*

51. EXT. DAY. OLIVIA'S HOUSE. THE FRONT FACADE.

OLIVIA (*impulsively following*):
  Unless, perchance, you come to me again
  To tell me how he takes it. Fare you well.
  I thank you for your pains. Spend this for me.
  OLIVIA *offers* CESARIO *money.*
CESARIO:
  I am no fee'd post, lady; keep your purse.
  My master, not myself, lacks recompense.
  Farewell, fair cruelty!
  CESARIO *makes the final disdainful remarks at a distance.*
  OLIVIA *follows to watch him kicking stones and walking*
  nonchalantly away. She slowly returns towards the main
  entrance of the house, turning furtively to glance at the
  retreating CESARIO.
OLIVIA:
  'What is your parentage?'

'Above my fortunes, yet my state is well.
I am a gentleman.' Nay. Not too fast! soft, soft –
Unless the master were the man. How now?
Even so quickly may one catch the plague?
Methinks I feel this youth's perfections,
With an invisible and subtle stealth,
To creep in at mine eyes. Well, let it be!

OLIVIA *reapproaches the house as* MALVOLIO *arrives to find out if the offensive young man is gone –* CESARIO *is almost at the gatehouse.*

OLIVIA:
What ho, Malvolio!

MALVOLIO:
Here, madam, at your service.

OLIVIA:
Run after that same peevish messenger,
The County's man. He left this ring behind him,
Would I or not. Tell him, I'll none of it.
Desire him not to flatter with his lord,
Nor hold him up with hopes; I am not for him.
If that the youth will come this way tomorrow,
I'll give him reasons for't.

MALVOLIO:
Madam, I will.

MALVOLIO *unhappy at the word 'run' – walks quickly after* CESARIO, *with the ring* OLIVIA *has given him.*

OLIVIA:
Hie thee, Malvolio!

MALVOLIO *does his unwilling best to quicken his pace as* OLIVIA *goes back to the house.*

OLIVIA:
I do I know not what, and fear to find
Mine eye too great a flatterer for my mind.
Fate, show thy force; ourselves we do not owe.
What is decreed must be, and be this so.

OLIVIA *runs inside the house, exhilarated by her own daring.*

52. EXT. LATE AFTERNOON. ESTATE COTTAGES.
MALVOLIO *commandeers a bicycle from outside an estate worker's cottage.*

53. EXT. DAY. COAST PATH.
CESARIO, *returning by the cliff path to* ORSINO's *castle, hears a bell ringing, stops and turns.* MALVOLIO *is wobbling on the bicycle towards her.* MALVOLIO *puts the bicycle down in the grass and approaches her.*

MALVOLIO: Were not you even now with the Countess Olivia?

CESARIO: Even now, sir; on a moderate pace I have since arrived but hither.

MALVOLIO: She returns this ring to you, sir. You might have saved me my pains, to have taken it away yourself. She adds, moreover, that you should put your lord into a desperate assurance she will none of him; and one thing more, that you be never so hardy to come again in his affairs – unless it be to report your lord's taking of this. Receive it so.

MALVOLIO *offers the ring to a bemused* CESARIO *whose attention has been caught by the wind tugging at what is now revealed as* MALVOLIO's *toupee.*

CESARIO: She took the ring of me? I'll none of it.

CESARIO *starts to walk away.*

MALVOLIO: Come, sir, you peevishly threw it to her, and her will is it should be so returned. If it be worth stooping for, there it lies in your eye; if not, be it his that finds it.

MALVOLIO *throws the ring down into the grass, turns the bicycle round and pedals away.* CESARIO *picks up the ring, examines it and gradually admits to the uneasy feeling that she is being propositioned.*

CESARIO:

I left no ring with her; what means this lady?
Fortune forbid my outside have not charmed her!
She made good view of me, indeed so much
That – methought – her eyes had lost her tongue,
For she did speak in starts, distractedly.
She loves me, sure, the cunning of her passion
Invites me in this churlish messenger.
None of my lord's ring? Why, he sent her none.
I am the man!

54. EXT. DAY. THE ROAD AND TAVERN BY A RIVER BANK AND QUAYSIDE.

Panoramically dropping down towards a river mouth and quayside, past a white-washed tavern from which, from the back view it seems CESARIO *is leaving. He is stopped by a demanding voice.*

ANTONIO *(V/O)*: Will you stay no longer?

He turns. It is not CESARIO *but* SEBASTIAN. *His interlocutor is in the doorway of the inn. It is* ANTONIO, *dressed in a big overcoat hiding his uniform.*

SEBASTIAN: By your patience, no.

ANTONIO: Let me yet know of you whither you are bound.

SEBASTIAN: No, sooth, sir.

SEBASTIAN *walks away towards the river and sits on a capstan looking out across the water.*

SEBASTIAN: You must know of me then, Antonio, my name is Sebastian. My father was that Sebastian of Messaline whom I know you have heard of. He left behind him

37

myself and a sister, Viola, both born in an hour – would we had so ended! But you, sir, altered that; before you took me from the breach of the sea was my sister drowned.

SEBASTIAN, *emotionally exhausted by his story, sobs in* ANTONIO'*s arms.*

ANTONIO: Alas the day!

SEBASTIAN: A lady, sir, though it was said she much resembled me, was yet of many accounted beautiful.

ANTONIO: Pardon me, sir, your bad entertainment.

SEBASTIAN: O good Antonio, forgive me your trouble.

ANTONIO *looks up as a coach approaches along the road.* SEBASTIAN *purposefully goes to wait for it, and when it stops he gets up on to one of the top passenger seats.*

ANTONIO: If you will not murder me for my love, let me be your servant.

SEBASTIAN: Desire it not. Fare ye well at once. I am bound to the Count Orsino's court. Farewell.

The coach rumbles away, watched by a grimly regretful ANTONIO.

ANTONIO:
The gentleness of all the gods go with thee!
I have many enemies in Orsino's court,
Else would I very shortly see thee there –

55. INT. NIGHT. ORSINO'S CASTLE. SMOKING ROOM.
ORSINO *is lighting a cheroot with a long match as he sits in a low armchair.*

ORSINO:
O when mine eyes did see Olivia first
Methought she purged the air of pestilence.
He leans over and lights another match for CESARIO'*s unwillingly held cheroot.* CESARIO *sucks in, goes green and*

tries very hard not to splutter as ORSINO *sinks back, closing his eyes.*

ORSINO:
   That instant was I turned into a hart
   And my desires like fell and cruel hounds
   E'er since pursue me.
   CESARIO *coughs out a cloud of smoke.*

56. EXT. NIGHT. OLIVIA'S HOUSE. GARDEN.
SIR TOBY *and* SIR ANDREW *are in the dark outside the walls surrounding* OLIVIA'*s property.* SIR TOBY *has got* SIR ANDREW *to form a ladder — and is climbing up him to the top of the wall — he half jumps, half falls to the ground below. He gets up, unbolts a small gate and peers out.*

SIR TOBY: Approach, Sir Andrew.
   There's nobody there ... Then there is a huge crash of breaking glass. SIR ANDREW *has climbed the wall and fallen off into a cucumber patch covered with glass panels.* SIR TOBY *comes back in and snorts with laughter, picks him up and they continue through garden.*
SIR TOBY: Not to be abed after midnight, is to be up early, and *diluculo surgere,* thou knowest —
SIR ANDREW: I know to be up late is to be up late.
SIR TOBY: A false conclusion! I hate it as an unfilled can. Do not our lives consist of the four elements?
SIR ANDREW: Faith, so they say; but I think it rather consists of eating and drinking.
SIR TOBY: Thou'rt a scholar. Let us therefore eat and drink.

57. EXT. NIGHT. OLIVIA'S HOUSE. GARDEN AND SIDE ENTRANCE.
SIR TOBY *throws stones up at* MARIA'*s window, two or three times.*

39

SIR TOBY: Marian, I say! A stoup of wine!

*SIR TOBY sits on the garden wall. SIR ANDREW joins him.
SIR TOBY hums. A figure approaches out of the dark across
the lawn and places a hand behind their two shoulders.*

FESTE: Did you never see the picture of We Three?

*They both yell – then see it is FESTE and howl with laughter.
SIR TOBY jumps up, clapping.*

58. INT. NIGHT. OLIVIA'S HOUSE. MARIA'S ROOM.

MARIA *goes to her window and peers down at the terrace.*

59. EXT. NIGHT. OLIVIA'S HOUSE. GARDEN AND SIDE ENTRANCE.

SIR TOBY: Welcome, ass! Now let's have a catch.

SIR ANDREW: Let our catch be 'Thou knave'.

FESTE: 'Hold thy peace, thou knave', knight? I shall be constrained in't to call thee knave, knight.

SIR ANDREW: Begin, fool; it begins 'Hold thy peace – '

FESTE: I shall never begin if I hold my peace.

SIR ANDREW: Good, i'faith. Come, begin!

They start the catch dancing round the croquet lawn, singing at the top of their voices.

Candlelight becomes visible inside the house and MARIA opens up the locks and bolts of the side door and emerges, dressed in a robe and nightdress.

MARIA: What a caterwauling do you keep here! If my lady have not called up her steward Malvolio, never trust me.

60. INT. NIGHT. OLIVIA'S HOUSE. CORRIDOR OUTSIDE
KITCHEN.

MARIA *urges them down the corridor towards the kitchen as*
SIR TOBY *yells back towards* MALVOLIO*'s room.*

SIR TOBY: My lady's a – Cataian; we are – politicians;
   Malvolio's a – Peg-a-Ramsey; and
      (*Sings.*) Three merry men be we!
   Am not I consanguineous? Am I not of her blood?

61. INT. NIGHT. OLIVIA'S HOUSE. MALVOLIO'S BEDROOM.
MALVOLIO, *sitting with brandy and reading a book of*
questionable content, looks up in annoyance.

62. INT. NIGHT. OLIVIA'S HOUSE. KITCHEN.

SIR TOBY: Tilly-vally! 'Lady'!
   MARIA *lights a lamp, as* SIR TOBY *searches for drink, finds*
   two sherry and port decanters, takes one and gives the other
   to SIR ANDREW.
FESTE: Beshrew me, the knight's in admirable fooling.
SIR TOBY (*sings*):
   There dwelt a man in Babylon, lady, lady –
SIR ANDREW: Ay, he does well enough if he be
disposed.
SIR TOBY (*sings*):
   Lady, lady –
SIR ANDREW: He does it with a better grace ...
SIR TOBY (*sings*):
   There dwelt a man in Babylon –
SIR ANDREW: ... but I do it more natural.
SIR TOBY (*sings*):
   There dwelt a man in Babylon –

SIR ANDREW (*as* FESTE *assists with the repartee*): By my troth, when thou spok'st of Pigrogromitus, of the Vapians passing the equinoctial of Queubus. 'twas very good, i'faith. I sent thee sixpence, hadst it?

FESTE *obliges – with snatches of operatic nonsense.*

FESTE: I did impetticoat thy gratillity; for Malvolio's nose is no whipstock, my lady has a white hand, and the Myrmidons are no bottle-ale houses.

SIR ANDREW: Excellent!

SIR ANDREW *falls backwards off his chair laughing.* SIR TOBY *goes to pick him up.*

SIR ANDREW: Now, a song!

SIR ANDREW *gets out a coin.* SIR TOBY *hands the coin to* FESTE *who expects a second, so* SIR ANDREW *gives him another.*

SIR TOBY: Come on, there is sixpence for you. Let's have a song.

63. INT. NIGHT. ORSINO'S HOUSE. DRAWING-ROOM.

ORSINO *is coming into a firelit room with just a few candles burning, as* CESARIO *plays the piano.*

ORSINO:
That old and antique song we heard last night.
Methought it did relieve my passion much.

CESARIO: He is not here, so please your lordship, that should sing it.

ORSINO: Who was it?

VALENTINE: Feste, my lord. A fool that the Lady Olivia's father took much delight in. He is about the house.

ORSINO: Seek him out, and play the tune the while.

64. INT. NIGHT. OLIVIA'S HOUSE. KITCHEN.

FESTE *has taken out his concertina and is sitting on the kitchen table.*

FESTE: Would you have a love song, or a song of good life?
SIR TOBY: A love song! A love song!
SIR ANDREW: Ay, ay, I care not for good life.
  SIR TOBY *and* SIR ANDREW *sit on chairs pulled up to the table as* MARIA *stands by the dresser.*
FESTE (*sings*):
  O mistress mine! Where are you roaming?
  O, stay and hear your true love's coming,
    That can sing both high and low.

65. INT. NIGHT. OLIVIA'S HOUSE. OLIVIA'S BEDROOM.

OLIVIA, *only half-asleep, propped up on pillows, comes out of a dreamy daze.*

66. INT. NIGHT. ORSINO'S CASTLE. SMOKING ROOM.

VALENTINE *has gone with the other cadets in search of* FESTE *and* CURIO *has taken over at the piano. He too is playing 'O Mistress Mine'. The fire crackles and sputters.* CESARIO *reaches forward to put a log back on the blaze.*

ORSINO:
  Come hither, boy.
  ORSINO *has gone to the card table and is dealing two hands of cards as* CESARIO *joins him. They smoke cigarettes.*
ORSINO:
  How dost thou like this tune?
CESARIO:
  It gives a very echo to the seat
  Where love is throned.
  ORSINO *is fascinated by this unusual delicate boy.*

43

ORSINO: Thou dost speak masterly.

67. INT. NIGHT. OLIVIA'S HOUSE. KITCHEN.

FESTE (*sings*):
    Trip no further, pretty sweeting;
    Journeys end in lovers meeting,
       Every wise man's son doth know.
SIR ANDREW: Excellent good, i'faith.
SIR TOBY: Good, good.
FESTE (*sings*):
    What is love? 'Tis not hereafter;
    Present mirth hath present laughter,

68. INT. NIGHT. ORSINO'S CASTLE. SMOKING ROOM.
ORSINO *starts to taunt* CESARIO *with the idea that he has fallen in love, but the joke is slightly uneasy, slightly jealous.*

ORSINO:
    My life upon't, young though thou art, thine eye
    Hath stayed upon some favour that it loves.
    Hath it not, boy?
CESARIO: A little, by your favour.
ORSINO:
    What kind of woman, is't?
CESARIO: Of your complexion.
ORSINO:
    She is not worth thee, then. What years, i'faith?
CESARIO:
    About your years, my lord.
ORSINO:
    Too old, by heaven. Let still the woman take
    An elder than herself; so wears she to him.

He becomes more whispered, even furtive, as he shares with
CESARIO *a real confessional bit of men's talk.*

ORSINO:

For, boy, however we do praise ourselves,
Our fancies are more giddy and unfirm,
More longing, wavering, sooner lost and worn,
Than women's are.

CESARIO: I think it well, my lord.

ORSINO:

Then let thy love be younger than thyself,
For women are as roses whose fair flower,
Being once displayed, doth fall that very hour.

CESARIO *turns away from* ORSINO *and tries to find a male
reaction to this male confidence.*

CESARIO:

And so they are. Alas, that they are so,
To die, even when they to perfection grow.
She tries to smile away her sadness.

69. INT. NIGHT. OLIVIA'S HOUSE. KITCHEN.
MARIA *joins* FESTE *singing.*

FESTE *and* MARIA:

What's to come is still unsure.

SIR TOBY *and* SIR ANDREW *listen fixed by* FESTE *as if he
is talking to them.* MARIA *sings to* SIR TOBY. *He catches her
eye.*

FESTE *and* MARIA:

In delay there lies no plenty –
Then come kiss me, sweet and twenty,
Youth's a stuff will not endure.

SIR ANDREW (*hushed and moved*): A mellifluous voice, as I
am true knight.

SIR TOBY *too understands the transience that* FESTE *has described and becomes sombre.*

SIR TOBY: A contagious breath.

SIR ANDREW: Very sweet and contagious, i'faith.

Then, SIR TOBY *gets up with a crash and leaps on to the table and becomes wild and a bit dangerous, grabbing a saucepan and ladle.*

SIR TOBY: But shall we make the welkin dance indeed? Shall we rouse the night-owl in a catch? Shall we do that?

SIR ANDREW: An you love me, let's do't.

SIR TOBY *begins to sing 'There dwelt a man' and leads a sort of conga out of the kitchen, followed by* MARIA *still trying to quieten them.*

70. INT. NIGHT. OLIVIA'S HOUSE. CORRIDOR.
The conga careens through the house.

71. INT. NIGHT. OLIVIA'S HOUSE. MALVOLIO'S BEDROOM.
MALVOLIO's *patience snaps. He gets up but checks himself on the way to the door as he remembers he is dressed uncharacteristically for his private fantasy in a flamboyant robe and silk breeches with yellow stockings.*

72. INT. NIGHT. OLIVIA'S HOUSE. MUSIC ROOM.
The door of the darkened room bursts open as the 'conga' crashes in. FESTE *goes to the piano and starts 'The Twelfth Day of December' – which becomes cacophonous and riotous.*

SIR TOBY *is dancing with* MARIA *and* SIR ANDREW *is dancing with a sofa bolster.* MARIA *gets free but* SIR TOBY *takes up with* SIR ANDREW *who suddenly puts a table cloth round his waist – and rejoins the dance –* SIR TOBY *grabs* MARIA *again.* SIR ANDREW *is doing a kind of solo tarantella.*

The door opens to reveal MALVOLIO *in dressing-gown,
pyjamas and carpet slippers.*

SIR TOBY (*sings*):
  O' the twelfth day of December –
MARIA: For the love o' God, peace!
  The piano stops – FESTE *stares in anticipation.* SIR
  ANDREW *dances on. As he sees* MALVOLIO *at last and
  stops, his 'skirt' drops to the floor.* MALVOLIO *advances into
  the room.* SIR TOBY *walks away and goes to sit down.*
MALVOLIO: My masters, are you mad? Or what are you? Do
  ye make an alehouse of my lady's house? Is there no
  respect of place, persons, nor time in you?
SIR TOBY: We did keep time, sir, in our catches. Sneck up!
  MALVOLIO *goes across the room to confront him.*
MALVOLIO: Sir Toby, I must be round with you. My lady
  bade me tell you that, though she harbours you as her
  kinsman, she's nothing allied to your disorders. If you can
  separate yourself and your misdemeanours, you are
  welcome to the house. If not, she is very willing to bid you
  farewell.
  SIR TOBY *sings in operetta-style across the room to* FESTE,
  who responds at the piano.
SIR TOBY (*sings*):
  Farewell, dear heart, since I must needs be gone –
MARIA: Nay, good Sir Toby!
FESTE (*sings*):
  His eyes do show his days are almost done –
MALVOLIO: Is't even so!
SIR TOBY (*sings*):
  But I will never die –
FESTE (*sings*):
  Sir Toby, there you lie –
MALVOLIO: This is much credit to you!

48

SIR TOBY *gets up and goes over to the piano, joining* FESTE *in a sort of chopsticks duet. As he does so* MARIA's *attention is caught by a small hint of yellow stocking peeping out from under* MALVOLIO's *nightgown.*

SIR TOBY (*sings*):
  Shall I bid him go?
FESTE (*sings*):
  What an if you do?
SIR TOBY (*sings*):
  Shall I bid him go and spare not?
FESTE (*sings*):
  O no, no, no, no, you dare not!
SIR TOBY: Out o'tune, sir, ye lie.

He stands up and walks more steadily than before to thrust his face inches from MALVOLIO's *nervous gaze.*

SIR TOBY: Art any more than a steward? Dost thou think, because thou art virtuous, there shall be no more cakes and ale?
FESTE: Yes, by Saint Anne, and ginger shall be hot i'the mouth, too.
SIR TOBY: Th'art i'the right. (*To* MALVOLIO.) Go, sir, rub your chain with crumbs. (*To* MARIA *firmly and quietly.*) A stoup of wine, Maria.

In the tension, she does a small curtsey and heads towards the next room. MALVOLIO *speaks his warning just as she opens the door.*

MALVOLIO: Mistress Mary, if you prize my lady's favour at anything more than contempt, you would not give means for this uncivil rule.

She stops for a moment, then continues.

  MALVOLIO *approaches the darkened room, where he can see her getting a bottle and glasses out of a cupboard. He goes, turning in the doorway.*

MALVOLIO: She shall know of it, by this hand!

  MALVOLIO *shuts the door after him.*

MARIA *appears in her doorway with the bottle and glasses.*

MARIA: Go, shake your ears.

SIR TOBY *and* FESTE *whoop with laughter; then* SIR ANDREW *catches on, as* SIR TOBY *releases a burst of dangerous anger.*

SIR TOBY: He's an overweening rogue. Bolts and shackles!

MARIA: Sweet Sir Toby, be patient for tonight.

SIR TOBY *and* SIR ANDREW *follow* MARIA *to a table, where she pours the wine. The three sit around the table in a huddled small group.*

MARIA: For Monsieur Malvolio, if I do not make him a common recreation, do not think I have wit enough to lie straight in my bed. I know I can do it.

SIR TOBY: Possess us, possess us, tell us something of him.

FESTE *slowly gets up and leaves the room.*

MARIA: Marry, sir, sometimes he is a kind of puritan –

SIR ANDREW: O, if I thought that, I'd beat him like a dog.

SIR TOBY (*genuinely perplexed at this vehemence*):
What, for being a puritan? Thy exquisite reason, dear knight?

SIR ANDREW (*trying not to retract*):
I have no exquisite reason for't, but I have reason good enough.

MARIA: The devil a puritan that he is, or anything, constantly, but a time-pleaser, so crammed, as he thinks, with excellencies, that it is his grounds of faith that all that look on him love him – and on that vice in him will my revenge find notable cause to work.

SIR TOBY: What wilt thou do?

MARIA *gets up.*

MARIA: I will drop in his way some obscure epistles of love; wherein, he shall find himself most feelingly personated.

73. INT. NIGHT. OLIVIA'S HOUSE. HALL/STAIRS.

MARIA *opens the drawer of a desk and shows her handwriting and a letter from* OLIVIA *to prove her point.*

MARIA: I can write very like my lady, your niece; on a forgotten matter we can hardly make distinction of our hands.

SIR TOBY: Excellent! I smell a device.

SIR ANDREW: I have't in my nose too.

MARIA: For this night, to bed –
She whispers, with self-conscious innuendo to SIR TOBY *but he shakes his head.*

MARIA (*trying to save face*): – and dream on the event. Farewell.
She goes upstairs with her candle, hurt and compromised.

SIR TOBY: Good night, Penthesilea.

SIR ANDREW: Before me, she's a good wench.
SIR ANDREW watches her, and then sits on the staircase.

SIR TOBY: She's a beagle true bred, and one that adores me – but what o'that?

SIR ANDREW: I was adored once, too.
SIR TOBY looks at him. SIR ANDREW's eyes are blurry with tears.

SIR TOBY: Let's to bed, knight.
SIR TOBY pats him on the shoulder and passes him on the way upstairs. SIR ANDREW doesn't move, but sits shivering slightly. SIR TOBY looks out of the landing window, and sees the dawn coming up.

SIR TOBY: Thou hadst need send for more money.

SIR ANDREW: If I cannot recover your niece, I am a foul way out.

SIR TOBY: Send for money, knight. If thou hast her not i'the end, call me cut.

SIR ANDREW: If I do not, never trust me, take it how you will.

SIR TOBY *looks up the stairs and then back at* SIR ANDREW. *Then he stumbles back down the stairs with the bottle.*

SIR TOBY: Come, come, I'll go burn some sack, 'tis too late to go to bed now. Come, knight; come, knight.

SIR ANDREW *gets up and follows* SIR TOBY *back into the ballroom.*

74. INT. DAWN. OLIVIA'S HOUSE. MARIA'S BEDROOM.
MARIA's *tear-stained face is glimpsed for an instant in the doorway listening to* SIR TOBY's *distant laughter before closing her door.*

75. INT. NIGHT. ORSINO'S HOUSE. CESARIO'S ATTIC ROOM.
CESARIO *is taking off the moustache and then the jacket and then the shirt. She stares into a small dressing-table mirror – a frail part-boy, part-girl with a vest covering her breasts.*

CESARIO:
Disguise, I see thou art a wickedness
Wherein the pregnant enemy does much.
How easy is it for the proper false
In women's waxen hearts to set their forms.
Alas, our frailty is the cause, not we,
For such as we are made of, such we be.
She picks up the photograph of SEBASTIAN *and explains her problems to her lost twin.*

CESARIO:
How will this fadge? My master loves her dearly;
And I, poor monster, fond as much on him;
And she, mistaken, seems to dote on me.
What will become of this? As I am man,
My state is desperate for my master's love.
As I am woman – now, alas the day,
What thriftless sighs shall poor Olivia breathe!

53

She goes to the window. She looks out at the moon and hears the sea.

CESARIO:

Time, thou must untangle this not I.

It is too hard a knot for me t'untie.

She closes the curtain and blows out the candle.

76. EXT. DAY. ORSINO'S ESTATE. FIELDS.

ORSINO *and five of his younger cadets, including* CESARIO, *are riding hard across open country by the sea. They all take a jump over a low hedge;* CESARIO *closes her eyes, cries of distress welling up in her.*

77. EXT. DAY. ORSINO'S CASTLE. BATHROOM.

ORSINO *is luxuriating in a hot tub of water in a steamy firelit room. He lies back and calls out.*

ORSINO:

Come hither, boy.

CESARIO *appears in the doorway and realizes she is in the most compromising situation so far.*

ORSINO:

Come fellow . . . come.

CESARIO *comes reluctantly to sit next to the bath, averting her gaze from its contents.*

ORSINO:

How will she love, when the rich golden shaft

Hath killed the flock of all affections else

That live in her . . .

ORSINO *sits up and offers* CESARIO *a sponge to wash his back with.*

ORSINO: . . . when brain and heart

Are all supplied with one self king!

54

CESARIO *caresses the back of the man she is becoming*
hopelessly attracted to but suddenly breaks off.

CESARIO:
Sir, shall I to this lady?
ORSINO *lies back.*

ORSINO: Ay, that's the theme
To her in haste.
CESARIO *in some relief stands up.*

ORSINO: Say,
My love can give no place, bide no denay.
CESARIO *bolts for the door.*

78. EXT. DAY. CLIFFS.
CESARIO *rides unwillingly towards* OLIVIA's *house.*

79. EXT. DAY. OLIVIA'S HOUSE. GARDEN.
MALVOLIO *is walking in the grounds.* MARIA *is watching him*
at a distance. He is faintly muttering and gesturing to himself.
He turns from the path he is on to another path fifty yards from
where MARIA *is half hidden. She looks across to the other side*
of the path. There is a box hedge enclosure surrounding a garden
statue adjacent to a sundial in the pathway. She darts across
the path and through some trees to a croquet lawn.

80. EXT. DAY. OLIVIA'S HOUSE. CROQUET LAWN.
SIR TOBY *and* SIR ANDREW *are playing croquet watched by*
the gardener's man, FABIAN, *who is working on an autumn*
bonfire, as MARIA *races down the bank towards them.*

MARIA: Malvolio's coming down this walk.
SIR TOBY *throws down his mallet and as* SIR ANDREW
sprints after MARIA, SIR TOBY *stops to insist* FABIAN
comes too.

55

SIR TOBY: Come thy ways, Signor Fabian. Wouldst thou not be glad to have the niggardly, rascally sheep-biter come by some notable shame?

FABIAN: You know he brought me out o'favour with my lady about a bear-baiting here.

They run to catch up the others.

81. EXT. DAY. OLIVIA'S HOUSE. GARDEN.

The plotters arrive at a vantage point where they can see MALVOLIO *lost in his own world.*

MARIA: He has been practising behaviour to his own shadow this half-hour. Get ye all three in the box-tree.

They scamper into the box-tree enclosure following MARIA. *Once they are installed she takes out the letter – and glances up the path to see* MALVOLIO *a few yards closer, still in the self-communing mode.*

    MARIA *stands in the pathway and lets the letter fall to her feet. Then she strolls away, whispering to the hidden three behind the hedge.*

MARIA: Here comes the trout that must be caught with tickling.

They peer through the leaves and see a fleeting impression of MALVOLIO'S *approach. He goes through the mime of kissing a woman's hand with a kind of allure.*

MALVOLIO: 'Tis but fortune, all is fortune. Maria once told me she did affect me; and I have heard herself come thus near, that should she fancy, it should be one of my complexion. Besides, she uses me with a more exalted respect than anyone else that follows her. What should I think on't?

    MALVOLIO *approaches the place where the conspirators are hidden. They hear him and whisper or mouth their responses.*

SIR ANDREW: 'Slight, I could so beat the rogue!

MALVOLIO: To be Count Malvolio ...

SIR TOBY: Ah, rogue!

MALVOLIO looks at the sundial, then takes out his pocket-watch. Clearly they don't agree. Instead of adjusting his watch, he applies pressure to the stone sundial and swivels it an inch from its axis.

SIR ANDREW (*in whispered hyperbole*): Pistol him, pistol him!

MALVOLIO sits at a stone garden seat in front of the box-hedge enclosure and plays out his most private of private fantasies.

MALVOLIO: Having been three months married to her, sitting in my state ...

SIR TOBY: O for a stone-bow to hit him in the eye!

MALVOLIO: Calling my officers about me, in my branched velvet gown, having come from a day-bed, where I have left Olivia sleeping ... And then after a demure travel of regard – telling them I know my place, as I would they should do theirs – to ask for my kinsman, Toby.

The conspirators, particularly SIR TOBY, fume.

SIR TOBY: Bolts and shackles!

MALVOLIO: I frown the while and perchance wind up my watch or play with my ... some rich jewel. Toby approaches, curtsies there to me; I extend my hand to him thus saying Cousin Toby, you must amend your drunkenness.

SIR TOBY: Out, scab!

MALVOLIO finally gets up and seeing the letter picks it up with a grudging cursory wheeze.

MALVOLIO: What employment have we here?

He looks briefly at it and places it on the garden seat. He walks away. SIR TOBY and FABIAN are deflated, SIR ANDREW confused. MALVOLIO stops. He is thinking about the letter. He returns and takes out his pince-nez.

MALVOLIO: By my life, this is my lady's hand. These be her very C's, her U's and her T's; and thus make she her great P's.

'To the unknown beloved this, and my good wishes.' Her very phrases!

He is first of all excited that he has found something which could get him praise from OLIVIA. *Then the phrase 'unknown beloved' begins to work on him.*

MALVOLIO: By your leave, wax. Soft! and the impressure her Lucrece, with which she uses to seal. 'Tis my lady! To whom should this be?

He takes the letter back to the seat he was on and discovers a poem written on the back of the envelope.

MALVOLIO (*reads*):
    'Jove knows I love;
      But who?
    Lips, do not move;
      No man must know.'

'No man must know'! If this should be thee, Malvolio!
    'I may command where I adore;
      But silence, like a Lucrece' knife,
    With bloodless stroke my heart doth gore;
      M.O.A.I. doth sway my life.

There is muffled delight, and attempts to see from inside the hedge, in the centre of which little space is a garden statue of a goddess, largely naked.

SIR TOBY: Excellent wench, say I!

MALVOLIO: 'M.O.A.I. doth sway my life.' Nay, but first let me see, let me see, let me see . . .

FABIAN: What dish o'poison has she dressed him!

MALVOLIO gets up and, pausing in the entrance to the box-hedge for a moment to see that he is not being overlooked, enters the nook and opens the letter. His pause has just given SIR TOBY, SIR ANDREW *and*

59

FABIAN *time to get out of the hedge through the opposite small gap.*

MALVOLIO: 'I may command where I adore'. Why, she may command me. I serve her, she is my lady. There is no obstruction in this. And the end: what should that alphabetical position portend? If I could make that resemble something in me ... Softly, 'M.O.A.I.' ... M ... Malvolio! M! Why, that begins my name! M! But then there is no consonancy in the sequel. 'A' should follow, but 'O' does. M.O.A.I. And yet, to crush this a little, it would bow to me, for every one of these letters are in my name. Soft! Here follows prose.

He is now more abandoned – putting on his glasses, reading fast aloud and with gathering excitement.

MALVOLIO (*reads*):

'If this fall into thy hand, revolve. In my stars I am above thee, but be not afraid of greatness. Some are born great, some achieve greatness, and some have greatness thrust upon 'em. Thy fates open their hands, let thy blood and spirits embrace them; and cast thy humble slough. Be opposite with a kinsman, surly with servants. Let thy tongue tang arguments of state. Put thyself into the trick of singularity. She thus advises thee that sighs for thee.'

He now stumbles over something that doesn't quite fit him as the mystery man, however much he wants it to.

MALVOLIO:

'Remember who commended thy yellow stockings and wished to see thee ever cross-gartered. I say, remember. Go to, thou art made if thou desirest to be so. If not, let me see thee a steward still ... (*All doubts now at an end.*) ... the fellow of servants, and not worthy to touch Fortune's fingers. Farewell. She that would alter services with thee, The Fortunate Unhappy.'

Daylight and champain discovers not more! This is open. I will be proud, I will read politic authors, I will baffle Sir Toby, I will wash off gross acquaintance, I will be point-devise the very man. I do not now fool myself, to let imagination jade me; for every reason excites to this, that my lady loves me.

SIR TOBY, SIR ANDREW and FABIAN on the other side of the hedge have ecstasies.

MALVOLIO celebrates with himself, circling round and round the statue, and eventually hugging it, allowing his hands to caress its contours in anticipation of the sexual delirium that is ahead of him.

MALVOLIO: I thank my stars, I am happy! I will be strange, stout, in yellow stockings and cross-gartered, even with the swiftness of putting on. Jove and my stars be praised!

He kisses the letter, and in doing so, sees there is another paragraph on the back of the page.

MALVOLIO: Here is yet a postscript.

(*Reads.*) 'Thou canst not choose but know who I am. If thou entertainst my love, let it appear in thy smiling, thy smiles become thee well. Therefore in my presence still smile, dear my sweet, I prithee.'

Jove, I thank thee! I will smile.

MALVOLIO works the muscles in his face, unused since childhood and through grimaces and sneers, finally arrives at a set and mirthless smile that would frighten dogs at a hundred paces.

MALVOLIO: I will do everything that thou wilt have me!

He stuffs the letter into his pocket and adjusting his clothes, he goes with uncharacteristic abandon up towards the house.

SIR TOBY, SIR ANDREW and FABIAN watch him go and rush hurtling through the garden towards the croquet lawn where MARIA is sitting on a bench.

FABIAN: I will not give my part of this sport for a pension of thousands.

SIR TOBY: I could marry this wench for this device.

SIR ANDREW: So could I too.

82. EXT. DAY. OLIVIA'S HOUSE. CROQUET LAWN.

SIR TOBY *extravagantly crawls across the lawn towards* MARIA, *collapsing full-length in front of her.* SIR ANDREW *does the same and gets caught up in a hoop.*

SIR TOBY: Wilt thou set thy foot o' my neck?

SIR ANDREW: Or o' mine either?

MARIA *is anxious to remain unobserved and quietens* SIR TOBY.

MARIA: Nay, but say true: does it work upon him?

SIR TOBY: Like aqua-vita with a midwife.

MARIA: Then mark his first approach before my lady ... he will come to her in yellow stockings, and 'tis a colour she abhors.

They all roar with laughter.

SIR ANDREW *laughs too until he realizes that* SIR TOBY *and* MARIA *are looking at him somewhat self-consciously.*

SIR ANDREW *is wearing a yellow cravat, yellow waistcoat, yellow socks and brown and yellow shoes.*

A bell rings up at the house. MARIA *urgently straightens her clothes and whispers.*

MARIA: Follow me.

SIR TOBY *picks up a mallet and wallops a croquet ball crashing through the flower beds, hurls down the mallet and whoops as he strides followed by* SIR ANDREW *up to the house.*

83. INT. DAY. OLIVIA'S HOUSE. DRESSING ROOM.

OLIVIA *is holding a black dress in front of her. She discards it and picks up another more* femme fatale *black dress. She discards it and picks up a pale blue dress. She smiles.*

84. EXT. DAY. OLIVIA'S ESTATE. STABLES.

CESARIO *is dismounting at the stables of* OLIVIA's *house. A groom leads the horse to the stalls and* CESARIO *walks up towards the house. She passes a gateway where* FESTE *is sitting on a mounting block playing a concertina.*

CESARIO: Save, thee, friend.

    FESTE *responds by putting his hand out for money.*

CESARIO: Dost thou live by thy music?

FESTE: No, sir, I live by the church.

CESARIO: Art thou a Churchman?

FESTE: No such matter, sir; I do live by the church. For I do live at my house, and my house doth stand by the church.

CESARIO: I warrant thou art a merry fellow, and car'st for nothing.

    CESARIO *sits alongside him.*

FESTE: Not so, sir. I do care for something; but in my conscience, sir, I do not care for you.

    He stares threateningly and searchingly at CESARIO.

FESTE: If that be to care for nothing, sir, I would it would make you invisible?

CESARIO: I saw thee late at the Count Orsino's.

FESTE: Foolery, sir, does walk about the orb like the sun, it shines everywhere. I think I saw your wisdom there?

    CESARIO *becomes uncomfortable and, getting up, takes out some money.*

CESARIO: Nay, an thou pass upon me ... Hold, there's expenses for thee!

CESARIO, *remembering a trick she would do with her brother, 'disappears' the coin as* FESTE *goes to take it. He grabs her hand and pulls her towards him.*

FESTE: Now Jove, in his next commodity of hair, send thee a beard!

Has he seen through her disguise? She struggles to contain her nervousness.

CESARIO: By my troth, I'll tell thee, I am almost sick for one though I would not have it grow on my chin. Is thy lady within?

FESTE *starts walking with her towards the house.*

FESTE: I would play Lord Pandarus of Phrygia, sir, to bring a Cressida to this Troilus.

CESARIO: I understand you, sir.

She quickly gives another coin.

FESTE: The matter, I hope, is not great, sir, begging but a beggar – Cressida was a beggar. My lady is within, sir. I will conster to them whence you come.

Leaving her outside on the gravel forecourt he goes up the steps and into the house.

CESARIO *shifts aimlessly for a few moments, looking at the house when her eye is caught by something.*

85. EXT. DAY. OLIVIA'S HOUSE. WINDOW.

MALVOLIO, *at a landing window is surveying the property and once every few seconds smiling in a sunburst of facial experiments.*

86. EXT. DAY. OLIVIA'S HOUSE. FORECOURT.

CESARIO *half looks behind her – who are these smiles for? – then tentatively acknowledges with a friendly wave.*

87. INT. DAY. OLIVIA'S HOUSE. WINDOW.
MALVOLIO *focuses on* CESARIO. *He scowls and turns his back to continue up the stairs.*

88. EXT. DAY. OLIVIA'S HOUSE. FORECOURT.
Perplexed, CESARIO *is squinting to see* MALVOLIO *when* SIR TOBY'*s voice rings out from the side of the house.*

SIR TOBY: Save you, gentleman!

CESARIO: And you, sir!

   SIR ANDREW *arrives too and assessing this to be a young nobleman, gives him a florid French greeting.*

SIR ANDREW: *Dieu vous garde, monsieur!*

CESARIO: *Et vous aussi; votre serviteur!*

   SIR ANDREW *is quickly out of his depth and returns to his native tongue.*

SIR ANDREW: I hope, sir, you are, and I am yours.

   SIR TOBY *intervenes indicating that* OLIVIA *wants to see* CESARIO *in her room at the back of the house.*

SIR TOBY: My niece is desirous you should enter, if your trade be to her.

CESARIO: Your niece, sir, is the list of my voyage.

   OLIVIA *and* MARIA *step out from the door* SIR TOBY *is approaching.*

CESARIO: But we are prevented. (*To* OLIVIA.) Most excellent, accomplished lady, the heavens rain odours on you!

SIR ANDREW (*to* SIR TOBY): That youth's a rare courtier. 'Rain odours'! Well!

   CESARIO *escorts* OLIVIA *towards the garden but seeing* SIR TOBY *and* SIR ANDREW *are still there, following them, she asks for privacy.*

CESARIO: My master hath no voice, lady, but to your own most pregnant and vouchsafed ear.

   SIR ANDREW *makes a note in a small pocket-book.*

SIR ANDREW: 'Odours'; 'pregnant'; and 'vouchsafed'. I'll
get 'em all three all ready.

89. EXT. DAY. OLIVIA'S GARDEN. ENTRANCE TO THE WALLED GARDEN.

OLIVIA *leads* CESARIO *towards the rear garden gate. At the
entrance, she turns to* MARIA.

OLIVIA: Let the garden door be shut.
   SIR ANDREW *noting things in a little book is unaware and
   follows them.* OLIVIA *suddenly turns with some impatience
   and condescension.*
OLIVIA: And leave me to my hearing.
   SIR ANDREW *is arrested by* OLIVIA'*s tone. He retreats,
   wanting to say something but unable to find the words.*

90. EXT. DAY. OLIVIA'S HOUSE. WALLED GARDEN.

OLIVIA *leads into the garden,* CESARIO *follows and* MARIA
shuts the door after them. They are alone. OLIVIA *asks to
shake hands as if to help* CESARIO'*s self-conciousness.*

OLIVIA:
   Give me your hand, sir.
CESARIO:
   My duty, madam, and most humble service!
   They stroll.
OLIVIA:
   What is your name?
CESARIO:
   Cesario is your servant's name, fair princess.
OLIVIA:
   Y'are servant to the Count Orsino, youth.
CESARIO:
   And he is yours, and his must needs be yours.

Your servant's servant is your servant, madam.

OLIVIA:

For him, I think not on him. For his thoughts,
Would, they were blanks rather than filled with me.

OLIVIA *sits at a small alfresco tea table she has had prepared for this interview.*

CESARIO:

I come to whet your gentle thoughts
On his behalf –

OLIVIA *asks* CESARIO *to sit down at the table and as she pours tea she makes her confession.*

OLIVIA:

Give me leave, beseech you. I did send,
After the last enchantment you did here,
A ring in chase of you. So did I abuse
Myself, my servant, and, I fear me, you.
To force that on you in a shameful cunning
Which you knew none of yours. What might you think?
Have you not set mine honour at the stake?
Let me hear you speak.

CESARIO:

I pity you.

OLIVIA: That's a degree to love.

CESARIO:

No, not a grize; for 'tis a vulgar proof
That very oft we pity enemies.

CESARIO *clumsily gets out the ring from a pocket and puts it on the table.* OLIVIA *looks at the ring, then* CESARIO, *and painfully accepts the rejection, putting the ring back on her own finger.*

OLIVIA:

Why, then, methinks 'tis time to smile again.
O world, how apt the poor are to be proud!

A clock strikes distantly.

OLIVIA:

The clock upbraids me with the waste of time.
Be not afraid, good youth; I will not have you.
She rises and begins the embarrassed walk back to the gate.

OLIVIA:

And yet, when wit and youth is come to harvest,
Your wife is like to reap a proper man.
There lies your way, due west.

CESARIO: Then westward ho!
*She stops on her way to the gate, remembering her
employment.*

CESARIO:

You'll nothing, madam, to my lord by me?
OLIVIA *races down the path.*

OLIVIA:

Stay.
I prithee, tell me what thou think'st of me?

CESARIO:

That you do think you are not what you are.

OLIVIA:

If I think so, I think the same of you.

CESARIO:

Then think you right; I am not what I am.

OLIVIA:

I would you were as I would have you be.
CESARIO *suddenly flashes in anger.*

CESARIO:

Would it be better, madam, than I am?
I wish it might, for now I am your fool.

OLIVIA:

O, what a deal of scorn looks beautiful
In the contempt and anger of his lip!
CESARIO *wheels round and heads for the gate again but as
she opens it* OLIVIA *slams it shut and hugs her forcing
CESARIO to flatten against the door.*

69

OLIVIA:

Cesario, by the roses of the spring,

By maidhood, honour, truth, and everything,

She becomes physically desperate, clutching CESARIO, *and sliding down to rest her head against* CESARIO'*s waist as she kneels beggingly in submission to her feelings.*

OLIVIA:

I love thee so that, maugre all thy pride,

Nor wit nor reason can my passion hide.

Desperate measures are necessary. CESARIO *untangles herself from the clasp and kneels next to* OLIVIA *and makes an oath or vow of what seems to be celibacy.*

CESARIO:

By innocence I swear, and by my youth,

I have one heart, one bosom, and one truth.

And that no woman has, nor never none

Shall mistress be of it, save I alone.

And so, adieu, good madam; never more

Will I my master's tears to you deplore.

She gets up and disappears through the garden gate. OLIVIA *stays down for a moment but then she rushes through the gateway and calls out to the departing* CESARIO.

OLIVIA:

Yet come again; for thou perhaps mayst move

That heart, which now abhors, to like his love.

CESARIO *pauses for a moment, but then strides on towards the stables.* OLIVIA *moans in despair and goes back through the gateway.*

SIR ANDREW *approaches to enter the garden for his turn.* OLIVIA *slams the door shut in his face. Shocked and hurt he walks aimlessly away.*

91. EXT. SUNSET. CAUSEWAY TO ORSINO'S CASTLE.
CESARIO *is riding slowly, at walking pace across the causeway
as the sun sets.*

92. EXT. SUNSET. TOWN MARKET PLACE.
Through a crowded thoroughfare of the fishing port beneath
ORSINO'S *castle thronging with vehicles, shoppers, fishermen
and stall-holders, weaves a uniformed young man with his back
to us, to all intents and purposes,* CESARIO. *He occasionally
half turns, senses something behind him and quickens his pace,
turning a corner and eventually ducking behind a parked cart.*

*The frock-coated figure who has been following him appears,
now half running, searching for his lost quarry, passing the cart.
The young man emerges. It is not* CESARIO *but* SEBASTIAN.
*Just as he is about to give his follower the slip, he looks back,
catches a glimpse of the man and stops in amazement. The man
walks forward, bespectacled and wearing a clerical collar.*
SEBASTIAN *looks questioningly. The man takes off the
spectacles and hat. It is* ANTONIO.

ANTONIO *leads them back to behind the cart, out of the
thoroughfare but still in view of the castle and they hug, which
for* ANTONIO *is clearly an emotional and physical sublimation.*

ANTONIO:
   I could not stay behind you.
   But not all love to see you – you sir are
   A stranger in these parts.
SEBASTIAN: My kind Antonio,
   I can no other answer make but thanks,
   And thanks. And ever oft good turns
   Are shuffled off with such uncurrent pay.
   SEBASTIAN *tries to distance* ANTONIO's *emotion just a
   little, looking at his guide book.*
SEBASTIAN (contd):
   I am not weary, and 'tis long to night.

71

I pray you, let us satisfy our eyes
With the memorials and the things of fame
That do renown this city.

The explanation for ANTONIO's *odd attire becomes*
apparent. ANTONIO's *hat and spectacles go back on.*

ANTONIO:

I do not without danger walk these streets.
Once in a seafight 'gainst Orsino's galleys
I did some service – of such note indeed
That, were I ta'en here, it would scarce be answered.

SEBASTIAN:

Belike you slew great number of his people?

ANTONIO:

For which, if I be lapsèd in this place,
I shall pay dear.

SEBASTIAN: Do not then walk too open.

ANTONIO:

You shall find me at the Elephant.

ANTONIO *designates a nearby inn and then offers a wallet of*
money to SEBASTIAN.

SEBASTIAN:

Why I your purse?

ANTONIO:

Haply your eye shall light upon some toy
You have desire to purchase; and your store,
I think, is not for idle markets, sir.

As they leave each other ANTONIO *needs to reassure himself*
that he will see SEBASTIAN *again and clasps him.*

ANTONIO:

At th'Elephant.

SEBASTIAN: I do remember.

ANTONIO *goes quickly into the crowd.* SEBASTIAN *watches*
him go with a reflective and perturbed look. Then he too
moves into the noisy street.

93. INT. NIGHT. ORSINO'S CASTLE. BILLIARD ROOM.
ORSINO *flexes his now nearly healed arm and surveys the billiard table.* CESARIO *stands uncomfortably behind him.*

ORSINO:
  If ever thou shalt love, remember me
  For such as I am, all true lovers are ...
  He takes his shot and misses badly.
ORSINO (*smiling*):
  Unstaid and skittish in all motions else,
  Save in the constant image of the creature
  That is beloved.
  As thunder rumbles distantly outside, CESARIO *now takes her shot, nervously and gawkily. After a spectacular double ricochet off two cushions, she sinks the black, looks at* ORSINO *and shrugs him a pallid smile.*

94. INT. NIGHT. A BARN NEAR THE SEA BELOW ORSINO'S CASTLE.
FESTE *is strumming and improvising a song in a corner of a darkened barn, which is his squat.*

95. EXT. NIGHT. ORSINO'S CASTLE. THE PATH TO THE SEA.
ORSINO *hurtles wildly down the path followed by* CESARIO *trying to keep up while carrying a hurricane lamp, as* FESTE'*s music, which they are seeking, gets louder.*

96. INT. NIGHT. THE BARN.
ORSINO *pushes open the door of the barn to discover* FESTE, *a bit the worse for drink, sitting on the straw.* FESTE *stops playing and begins to recoil from what he assumes is arrest but* ORSINO *calms him and perches on the wheel of a farm cart, beckoning* CESARIO *to join him.*

74

ORSINO:

O, fellow, come, the song we had last night.

Mark it, Cesario; it is old and plain.

CESARIO *hangs the oil lamp from the cart. It swings eerily as* FESTE *starts the song.*

ORSINO:

Prithee sing.

CESARIO *creeps away to lean against the straw a few feet away from* ORSINO.

FESTE *sings plangently, closing his eyes.*

FESTE (*sings*):

Come away, come away, death,

And in sad cypress let me be laid.

Fly away, fly away, breath!

I am slain by a fair cruel maid.

ORSINO *rests his head back in a melancholy mood at the achingly sad song. But he realizes he is missing something.*

FESTE (*sings*):

My shroud of white, stuck all with yew,

O, prepare it!

My part of death, no one so true

Did share it.

CESARIO *sees* ORSINO's *state and turns away.*

ORSINO *looks for* CESARIO. *As the first verse ends, he moves to stand behind* CESARIO. *He whispers an explanation of the song.*

ORSINO:

The spinners, and the knitters in the sun,

Do use to chant it. It is silly sooth,

And dallies with the innocence of love

Like the old age.

CESARIO *is highly aware of* ORSINO's *mouth at her ear.*

ORSINO's *face doesn't go away, he takes* CESARIO's *hand, while listening, almost luxuriating in the melancholy.*

FESTE (*sings*):

> Not a flower, not a flower sweet
>> On my black coffin let there be strewn.

CESARIO *is yearningly aroused – and begins slowly, slowly to turn her head towards* ORSINO's *mouth.*

FESTE (*sings*):

> Not a friend, not a friend greet
>> My poor corpse where my bones shall be thrown.
> A thousand thousand sighs to save,
>> Lay me, O, where
> Sad true lover never find my grave
>> To weep there.

ORSINO *and* CESARIO *look at each other for a moment, startled by what they are doing and the absence of music.*

FESTE *stares.* ORSINO *throws a coin to* FESTE.

ORSINO: There's for thy pains.

FESTE's *eye glitters with a sort of understanding.*

FESTE: No pains, sir. I take pleasure in singing.

ORSINO: I'll pay thy pleasure, then.

FESTE: Truly, sir, and pleasure will be paid, one time or another.

ORSINO *is aware that something has almost happened between him and the boy, and he curtly excuses himself to* FESTE.

ORSINO: Give me now leave, to leave thee.

97. EXT. NIGHT. ORSINO'S HOUSE. DOORWAY/BARN.

CESARIO *runs after* ORSINO *as* FESTE *comes to the door of the barn and calls after him.*

FESTE: Now the melancholy god protect thee for thy mind is a very opal. I would have men of such constancy put to sea, that their business might be everything, and their intent everywhere; for that's it that always makes a good voyage of nothing. Farewell.

77

98. EXT. NIGHT. CLIFF AND SEA.

ORSINO *is heading towards a bluff that overlooks the sea.*
Thunder rumbles and crashes. He stands, windblown and
distressed, keeping his back to CESARIO.

ORSINO:

    Once more, Cesario,

    Get thee to yond same sovereign cruelty.

    CESARIO *turns away in despair.*

ORSINO:

    Tell her my love, more noble than the world,

    Prizes not quantity of dirty lands.

    But 'tis that miracle and queen of gems

    That nature pranks her in, attracts my soul.

CESARIO:

    But if she cannot love you, sir?

ORSINO (*angrily*):

    I cannot so be answered.

CESARIO (*shouting in exasperation against the wind*):

                   Sooth, but you must.

    Say that some lady, as perhaps there is,

    Hath for your love as great a pang of heart

    As you have for Olivia. You cannot love her.

    You tell her so. Must she not then be answered?

    The waves crash below them. ORSINO *looks suicidal as he*
    anguishes over the concept of rejection and turns
    contemptuously on his young companion.

ORSINO:

    There is no woman's sides

    Can bear the beating of so strong a passion

    As love doth give my heart; no woman's heart

    So big to hold so much, they lack retention.

    Alas, their love may be called appetite,

    But mine is all as hungry as the sea,

    And can digest as much. Make no compare

Between that love a woman can bear me
And that I owe Olivia.

CESARIO: Ay, but I know –
The argument becomes dangerous. ORSINO *loses his temper*
with CESARIO *who nevertheless faces him out.*

ORSINO: What dost thou know?

CESARIO:

Too well what love women to men may owe.
In faith, they are as true of heart as we.
My father had a daughter loved a man –
As it might be perhaps, were I a woman,
I should your lordship.

CESARIO moves away to sit on a rock. He follows her, again
in spite of himself, mesmerised.

ORSINO: And what's her history?
She is within a breath of confessing her real identity.

CESARIO:

A blank, my lord. She never told her love,
But let concealment, like a worm i'the bud,
Feed on her damask cheek. She pined in thought,
And with a green and yellow melancholy,
She sat like Patience on a monument,
Smiling at grief. Was not this love indeed?
We men may say more, swear more, but indeed
Our shows are more than will; for still we prove
Much in our vows, but little in our love.
She gets up and starts to leave, unable to maintain the
deception any more.

ORSINO:

But died thy sister of her love, my boy?

CESARIO:

I am all the daughters of my father's house,
And all the brothers too; and yet, I know not ...
CESARIO goes. ORSINO *turns back to look at the sea. He*
will not sleep tonight. The waves crash on the rocks.

99. EXT. MORNING. ORSINO'S HOUSE. TERRACE.
CESARIO *is emerging from* ORSINO'*s castle and sees* ORSINO *standing huddled on the battlements.*

CESARIO:
  I'll do my best to woo your lady.
  ORSINO *doesn't respond.* CESARIO *turns away and walks down the steps.* ORSINO *looks almost guiltily after the boy who is consuming his thoughts.* CESARIO'*s thoughts are similarly hidden.*
CESARIO (*V/O*):
  And yet a barful strife.
  Who e'er I woo, myself would be his wife.

100. EXT. MORNING. MARKET TOWN. STREET.
SEBASTIAN, *consulting his ever present Baedeker guide book sets off early for his day of sight-seeing.*

101. EXT. MORNING. CAUSEWAY WITH ORSINO'S CASTLE IN THE DISTANCE.
CESARIO *strides out on her now familiar go-between route.*

102. EXT. MORNING. SHORELINE OPPOSITE ORSINO'S CASTLE.
SEBASTIAN, *dressed identically to* CESARIO *we may notice, is heading along the mainland towards* OLIVIA'*s house.*

103. EXT. MORNING. MARKET TOWN. HOTEL.
ANTONIO *comes out of the Elephant Hotel in a great hurry, dressed in his disguise, looking anxiously for* SEBASTIAN. *He runs slap into two soldiers, the crash knocks his hat off and his glasses smash on the pavement. He looks up as one of the soldiers is picking up his hat and apologizing, to see that the other is*

80

narrowing his eyes in recognition. He accepts the hat, ignores the glasses and moves away into the crowd. The soldier stares after him. ANTONIO *sees the soldier, having alerted the other one, is coming after him, and in an attempt to get away from them,* ANTONIO *begins to run. The soldiers give chase down an alley, through a maze of washing and down another alley. Shots are fired as three other soldiers arrive.*

ANTONIO *collides disastrously with a fish porter, knocking him and his fish to the ground. The pursuing soldiers skid and flounder.*

Finally ANTONIO *crawls into the back of a horse-drawn wagon heading out of town, as the distant soldiers fret, and then confer with two other soldiers who spring into action.*

104. INT. DAY. OLIVIA'S HOUSE. STAIRS/HALL.
Crashing down the main stairs of OLIVIA'*s house carrying a birdcage and a violin case comes* SIR ANDREW *followed in a flurry by* FABIAN *and two porters laden with two suitcases, a hat-box and an assortment of tennis racquets, golf clubs, boxing gloves, cricket pads and a selection of foils and fighting swords.* SIR TOBY *obviously caught by this crisis while shaving, brings up the rear.* SIR ANDREW *is leaving.*

SIR ANDREW: No, faith, I'll not stay a jot longer.
   The conversation hurtles down two flights of stairs, through the hall and to a waiting pony and trap which is to take SIR ANDREW *to the station.*
SIR TOBY: Thy reason, dear venom, give thy reason.
SIR ANDREW: Marry, I saw your niece do more favours to the Count's servingman than ever she bestowed upon me. I saw't i'the garden.
SIR TOBY: Did she see thee the while, old boy, tell me that?
SIR ANDREW: As plain as I see you now.

FABIAN: This was a great argument of love in her toward you.

SIR ANDREW *turns scornfully on this suggestion.*

SIR ANDREW: 'Slight! Will you make an ass o'me?

SIR TOBY *encourages* FABIAN *to explain.*

FABIAN: She did show favour to the youth in your sight only to exasperate you, to awake your dormouse valour. You should then have accosted her, and banged the youth into dumbness. You are now sailed into the north of my lady's opinion, unless you do redeem it by some laudable attempt either of valour or policy.

At the last minute, SIR ANDREW *relents and clambering down begins under* SIR TOBY's *guidance to return to the house through the hall to the stairs.*

SIR ANDREW: It must be with valour, for policy I hate. I had as lief be a puritan as a politician.

SIR TOBY: Why then ... Challenge me the Count's youth to fight with him; hurt him in eleven places; my niece shall take note of it – and there is no love-broker in the world can more prevail with woman than report of valour.

Suddenly, SIR ANDREW *is resolved.*

SIR ANDREW: Will either of you bear me a challenge to him?

SIR TOBY: Go, write it in a martial hand. Be curst and brief. It is no matter how witty, so it be eloquent.

SIR ANDREW *runs back for one of the smaller cases, with* SIR TOBY *urging him not to delay.*

SIR TOBY: About it! Taunt him with the licence of ink!

SIR ANDREW: Where shall I find you?

SIR TOBY: We'll call thee at thy cubiculo. Go!

SIR ANDREW *runs back up the stairs to his room.*

FABIAN: This is a dear manikin to you, Sir Toby.

SIR TOBY: I have been dear to him, lad, some two thousand strong or so.

They are coming down into the hallway when MARIA
appears speeding down the stairs behind them. MARIA *is
convulsed; her eyes indicate upstairs.*

MARIA (*whispering*): Yond gull Malvolio is turned heathen.
He's in yellow stockings!

SIR TOBY: And cross-gartered?

The doorway to the drawing-room opens. It is OLIVIA, *who
sees and hears* MARIA *and* SIR TOBY *laughing.*

OLIVIA:
Where's Malvolio? He is sad and civil.
And suits well for a servant with my fortunes.

105. INT. DAY. OLIVIA'S HOUSE. DRAWING ROOM.

SIR TOBY *retreats as* MARIA *goes with* OLIVIA *back into the
drawing-room.*

MARIA: He's coming, madam, but in very strange manner.

OLIVIA: Why, what's the matter?

MARIA: Madam, your ladyship were best to have some
guard about you.

OLIVIA: Go, call him hither.

OLIVIA *is left alone. She walks about for a moment and then
settles in a chair by the window.*

*There is a tap on the door. The door opens. There is a high-
backed sofa between* OLIVIA *and the door.* MALVOLIO's *face
appears. He glances around the room, sees they are alone and
then gives* OLIVIA *a look intended to be sulphurously alluring.*

OLIVIA: How now, Malvolio?

MALVOLIO: Sweet lady! Ho! Ho!

*With passionate confirmation he steps from behind the sofa to
reveal breeches to the knee and scintillating yellow stockings
tied up with black silk ribbons. He displays the full effect and
climaxes the moment with a crazed fixed smile.*

OLIVIA: Smil'st thou? I sent for thee upon a sad occasion.

MALVOLIO: Sad, lady? I could be sad; this does make some
obstruction in the blood, this cross-gartering – but what of
that?

*He comes closer to her putting in a twirl for her delectation,
and adding to the smile with the occasional wink.*

MALVOLIO: If it please the eye of one, 'Please one and
please all'.

OLIVIA: Why, how dost thou, man? What is the matter with
thee?

MALVOLIO: Not black in my mind, though yellow in my
legs. It did come to his hands; and commands shall be
executed.

MALVOLIO *kneels with excruciating difficulty in front of her
and takes her hand. He kisses her hand.* OLIVIA, *aghast,
considers calling for help.*

MALVOLIO: I think we do know the sweet Roman hand.

OLIVIA *feels* MALVOLIO'*s forehead temperature, fearing a
fever.*

OLIVIA: Wilt thou go to bed, Malvolio?

MALVOLIO: To bed!

He hauls himself up to beside OLIVIA *in passionate
whispered confirmation of a tryst in her bedroom.*

MALVOLIO: 'Ay, sweetheart, and I'll come to thee!'

*He blows kisses to her in a heavy-lidded seductive way and
then flashes another shattering smile.*

OLIVIA: God comfort thee! Why dost thou smile so, and kiss
thy hand so oft?

MARIA *comes into the drawing-room, leaving* SIR TOBY *and
FABIAN in the hallway and plays at being shocked and full
of worried concern.*

MARIA: How do you, Malvolio? Why appear you with this
ridiculous boldness before my lady?

MALVOLIO *continues to have a private hushed* tête-à-tête,
while occasionally gesturing for MARIA *to go away.*

MALVOLIO: 'Be not afraid of greatness.' 'Twas well writ.

OLIVIA: What mean'st thou by that, Malvolio?

MALVOLIO: 'Some are born great – '

OLIVIA: Ha?

MALVOLIO: 'Some achieve greatness –'

OLIVIA: What sayst thou?

MALVOLIO: 'And some have greatness thrust upon them.'

OLIVIA is retreating from MALVOLIO*'s ecstatic lunges, as he follows her on his knees.*

OLIVIA: Heaven restore thee!

MALVOLIO: 'Remember who commended thy yellow stockings – '

OLIVIA: Thy yellow stockings?

MALVOLIO: '– and wished to see thee cross-gartered.'

OLIVIA: Cross-gartered?

MALVOLIO: 'Go to, thou art made if thou desir'st to be so.'

OLIVIA: Am I made!

MALVOLIO: 'If not, let me see thee a servant still.'

OLIVIA, alarmed and bothered, cannot stop herself from seeing the funny side of this outburst.

OLIVIA: Why, this is very midsummer madness.

From outside the window on the terrace, one of the gardeners calls out.

SERVANT: Madam, the young gentleman of the Count Orsino's is returned.

OLIVIA grasps her chance to escape this bizarre encounter with her butler.

OLIVIA: I'll come to him.

She pauses in the doorway to look back at the chuckling, smiling MALVOLIO *who is still on his knees blowing kisses and instructs* MARIA, *partly for* MALVOLIO*'s benefit, before leaving the room and running outside.*

OLIVIA: Good Maria, let this fellow be looked to. Where's my cousin Toby? Let some of my people have a special care of him.

MALVOLIO *jumps up with a great cry of delight and triumph that sends* MARIA *retreating round the room and finally rushing away through the door to the hall.*

MALVOLIO: O ho! Do you come near me now? No worse man than Sir Toby to look to me! She sends him on purpose, that I may appear stubborn to him.

He talks to himself, occasionally consulting the already worn and crumpled letter; while circling the room, looking into the mirror, sitting in chairs and clenching his fist in ugly, febrile triumph.

MALVOLIO: I have limed her! But it is Jove's doing, and Jove make me thankful! And when she went away now – 'let this fellow be looked to'. Fellow! Not 'Malvolio', nor after my degree, but 'fellow'! Why, everything adheres together, no obstacle, no incredulous or unsafe circumstance – what can be said? –

He looks through the window and sees OLIVIA *crossing the lawn with* CESARIO.

MALVOLIO: – nothing that can be, can come between me and the full prospect of my hopes.

106. INT. DAY. OLIVIA'S HOUSE. THE HALL.
SIR TOBY *is waiting in the hallway as if having been summoned by* MARIA *– who is helping him on with his jacket.* FABIAN *stands on the stairs as* MALVOLIO *emerges from* OLIVIA's *drawing-room.*

SIR TOBY: In the name of sanctity, if all the devils of hell possessed him, I'll speak to him.

FABIAN: How is't with you, sir?

MALVOLIO: Go off, I discard you. Let me enjoy my private. Go off.

MALVOLIO *avoids* SIR TOBY *and* MARIA *and turns up the side stairs into a small library.*

107. INT. DAY. OLIVIA'S HOUSE. LIBRARY.

MARIA, SIR TOBY *and* FABIAN *follow him into the library.*
MALVOLIO *opens a cabinet and examines various books while they whisper about him.*

MARIA: Did not I tell you? Sir Toby, my lady prays you to have a care of him.
MALVOLIO: Ah ha! Does she so!
SIR TOBY: Go to, go to! Peace, peace, we must deal gently with him. Let me alone. How do you, Malvolio? How is't with you? What, man, defy the devil!
MALVOLIO: Do you know what you say?
MARIA: La you, an you speak ill of the devil, how he takes it at heart! Pray God he be not bewitched!
FABIAN: Carry his water to the wisewoman.
MARIA: It shall be done tomorrow morning. My lady would not lose him, for more than I'll say.
MALVOLIO: How now, mistress?
MARIA: O Lord!

108. INT. DAY. OLIVIA'S HOUSE. HALL/STAIRS.

SIR TOBY: Prithee, hold thy peace, this is not the way. Let me alone with him.
FABIAN: No way but gentleness, gently, gently.
They surround MALVOLIO *on the stairs.*
SIR TOBY: Why, how now, my bawcock? How dost thou, chuck?
MALVOLIO: Sir!
SIR TOBY: What, man, 'tis not for gravity to play at cherry-pit with Satan.
MARIA: Get him to say his prayers, good Sir Toby; get him to pray.
MALVOLIO: My prayers, minx!

MARIA: No, I warrant you, he will not hear of godliness.

He continues past them up the stairs, finally delivering his dismissal of them from in every sense a great height.

MALVOLIO: Go, hang yourselves all. You are idle, shallow things; I am not of your element. You shall know more hereafter.

FABIAN, MARIA and SIR TOBY walk soberly away to the hallway where they explode and collapse with laughter.

SIR TOBY: Is't possible?

FABIAN: If this were played upon a stage now, I would condemn it as an improbable fiction.

SIR TOBY hugs MARIA who clasps on to him, but he breaks the embrace.

SIR TOBY looks up the stairs towards MALVOLIO's room and gets a strange malignant glint in his eye.

SIR TOBY: Come, we'll have him in a dark room and bound.

MARIA: Why, we shall make him mad indeed.

SIR TOBY: My niece is already in the belief that he's mad. We may carry it thus for our pleasure and his penance.

He stills the laughter of the others with his dangerously excited anticipation of blood sport. MARIA *looks troubled.*

They look up, hearing odd angry sotto *words coming from somewhere above them.*

Emerging on the landing above them is SIR ANDREW *reading to himself but enacting his challenge.*

FABIAN: More matter for a May morning!

SIR ANDREW whirls round, sees them looking at him and comes plunging down the stairs with his page of writing.

SIR ANDREW: Here's the challenge, read it. I warrant there's vinegar and pepper in't.

FABIAN: Is't so saucy?

SIR ANDREW: Ay, is't, I warrant him. Do but read.

SIR TOBY: Give me.

SIR TOBY sits with the paper at a small table and gets out a fountain pen in case he needs to make corrections – like a

teacher marking homework. Meanwhile, FABIAN *stands guard in case they are overheard.*

SIR TOBY: 'Youth, whatsoever thou art, thou art but a scurvy fellow.'

FABIAN: Good and valiant.

First one and then three maids congregate upstairs looking over the bannister and see SIR ANDREW *enacting his forthcoming confrontation.*

SIR TOBY: 'Thou com'st to the Lady Olivia, and in my sight she uses thee kindly. But thou liest in thy throat; that is not the matter I challenge thee for.'

FABIAN: Very brief, and to exceeding good sense – (*To himself.*) less!

SIR TOBY: 'I will waylay thee going home; where, if it be thy chance to kill me – '

FABIAN: Good!

SIR TOBY: 'thou kill'st me like a rogue and a villain.'

FABIAN: Still you keep o' the windy side of the law; good.

SIR TOBY: 'Fare thee well, and God have mercy upon one of our souls. He may have mercy upon mine, but my hope is better – and so, look to thyself. Thy friend ... '

SIR TOBY *is perplexed when the challenge appears to end 'thy friend'. He looks up aghast.* SIR ANDREW *comes over and turns the page and* SIR TOBY *sees that the writing continues.*

SIR TOBY: ' ... as thou usest him, and thy sworn enemy. Andrew Aguecheek.' If this letter move him not, his legs cannot. I'll give't him.

As SIR TOBY *finishes the letter, he puts away his pen, gets up and surges through the hall towards the drawing-room, followed by* SIR ANDREW, MARIA *and* FABIAN.

MARIA *overtakes* SIR TOBY *and points out where* OLIVIA *and* CESARIO *have gone distantly in the garden.*

MARIA: He is now in some commerce with my lady.

90

SIR TOBY *assesses the situation and, doing up* SIR
ANDREW's *sword belt a bit tighter he directs him to the
orchard which is well away from* CESARIO.

SIR TOBY: Go, Sir Andrew. Scout me for him at the corner
of the orchard like a bum-baily. So soon as ever thou seest
him, draw, and as thou drawest, swear horrible; Away!

SIR ANDREW *goes martially, only slightly encumbered by
the sword thwacking his calves.*

SIR ANDREW: Nay, let me alone for swearing.

SIR TOBY *watches* SIR ANDREW *go, and then tears up the
letter depositing the bits in a waste-basket.*

SIR TOBY: I will deliver his challenge by worth of mouth.

109. EXT. DAY. OLIVIA'S HOUSE. THE SUNKEN GARDEN.
OLIVIA *and* CESARIO *have reached a fountain near the box
tree.* CESARIO *sits on the stone wall next to* OLIVIA, *hands in
pockets, in a resentful mood.* OLIVIA *throws petals into the
water. The talk is desultory.*

OLIVIA:
I have said too much unto a heart of stone,
Suddenly OLIVIA *turns and offers* CESARIO *a small locket
and when it is rejected, she becomes childlike and petulant.*
OLIVIA:
Here, wear this jewel for me, 'tis my picture.
Refuse it not, it hath no tongue to vex you.
And I beseech you, come again tomorrow.
What shall you ask of me that I'll deny.
CESARIO *arrives at a similar tone, two schoolgirls
quarrelling.*
CESARIO:
Nothing but this; your true love for my master.

91

OLIVIA:
  How with mine honour may I give him that
  Which I have given to you?
CESARIO: I will acquit you.

110. EXT. DAY. OLIVIA'S ESTATE. THE MONUMENT.
FESTE *is leaning against a monument, barnacled with cupids
and goddesses, with* OLIVIA'*s house considerably in the
distance. Looking at the monument, still armed with his
guidebook is* SEBASTIAN.

SEBASTIAN (*V/O*): You are a foolish fellow.
FESTE:
  Will you make me believe that I am not sent for you?
SEBASTIAN:
  Go to.

111. EXT. DAY. OLIVIA'S HOUSE. THE SUNKEN GARDEN.
OLIVIA *stands up and runs off. She calls her last desperate line
from the steps leading back to the house.*

OLIVIA:
  Well, come again tomorrow. Fare thee well.
  A fiend like thee might bear my soul to hell.
  CESARIO *hangs her head moaning in exasperation and then
  walks resolutely off down the lane leading to the orchard.*

112. EXT. DAY. OLIVIA'S ESTATE. THE MONUMENT.
SEBASTIAN *curtly dismisses* FESTE *as a tramp and strides off
downhill towards the house.*

SEBASTIAN: Let me be clear of thee.
FESTE: Well held out.

CESARIO *is walking away from the house when* SIR TOBY *comes from behind a hedge and salutes her.*

SIR TOBY: Gentleman, God save thee!

CESARIO: And you, sir.

SIR TOBY: That defence thou hast, betake thee to't. Of what nature the wrongs are thou hast done him, I know not; but thy intercepter, full of despite, bloody as the hunter, attends thee at the orchard end.

SIR TOBY *guides* CESARIO *into the area of the orchard, where dimly distant through the trees,* SIR ANDREW *is visible.*

CESARIO: You mistake, sir. I am sure no man hath any quarrel to me.

SIR TOBY: You'll find it otherwise, I assure you. Therefore, if you hold your life at any price, betake you to your guard; for your opposite hath in him what youth, strength, skill, and wrath can furnish man withal.

CESARIO: I pray you, sir, what is he?

SIR TOBY: He is a devil in private brawl. Souls and bodies hath he divorced three; and his incensement at this moment is so implacable, that satisfaction can be none, but by pangs of death, and sepulchre.

CESARIO: I will return again into the house and desire some conduct of the lady.

CESARIO *makes a break for it back to the house but* FABIAN *appears from nowhere to cut off the exit and* SIR TOBY *quite brutally restrains her.*

CESARIO (*suddenly angry*): I am no fighter. I beseech you, to know of the knight what my offence to him is. It is something of my negligence, nothing of my purpose.

SIR TOBY: I will do so. Signor Fabian, stay you by this gentleman till my return.

CESARIO *tries to find out more about 'the quarrel' as*
FABIAN *encourages her closer to* SIR ANDREW *through the*
trees.

CESARIO: Pray you, sir, do you know of this matter?

FABIAN: I know the knight is incensed against you, even to a
mortal arbitrement, but nothing of the circumstance
more.

114. EXT. DAY. OLIVIA'S ESTATE. THE FAR END OF THE
ORCHARD WALL.

SIR TOBY *is clattering through branches and thick grass*
approaching SIR ANDREW.

SIR TOBY: Why, man, he's a very devil. I have not seen such
a firago. I had a pass with him and he gives me the stuck-
in with such a mortal motion that it is inevitable. They say
he has been fencer to the Shah of Persia.

SIR ANDREW: Pox on't! I'll not meddle with him.

SIR ANDREW *is moved closer to the middle of the orchard by*
SIR TOBY *and can see through the thick branches the bottom*
half of his chosen opponent.

SIR TOBY: Ay, but he will not now be pacified. Fabian can
scarce hold him yonder.

SIR ANDREW: Plague on't! Let him let the matter slip, and
I'll give him my horse.

SIR TOBY: I'll make the motion. Stand here, make a good
show on't. (*To himself, as he walks back to* FABIAN.) I'll
ride your horse as well as I ride you!

CESARIO *is beginning visibly to panic and* FABIAN *takes*
the opportunity to wind her up.

CESARIO: I beseech you, what manner of man is he?

FABIAN: Nothing by his form, as you are like to find him in
the proof of his valour. I will make your peace with him, if
I can.

CESARIO: I shall be much bound to you for't.

SIR TOBY *is returning through the branches and meets up with* FABIAN. *The two assailants are now only thirty feet apart.*

SIR TOBY: I have persuaded him the youth's a devil.

FABIAN: He is as horribly conceited of him.

The referees part again and go to speak to their opposite fighters, and then return to those they were seconding.

SIR TOBY: There's no remedy, sir, he will fight with you for's oath's sake. Therefore, draw.

CESARIO (*to herself*): Pray God defend me! A little thing would make me tell them how much I lack of a man.

FABIAN: Give ground if you see him furious.

SIR TOBY (*crossing to* SIR ANDREW): Come, Sir Andrew, there's no remedy. The gentleman will, for his honour's sake, have one bout with you.

Finally, CESARIO *and* SIR ANDREW *are in the clearing at the centre of the orchard and draw their swords –* SIR ANDREW'*s with the scabbard still on.* SIR TOBY *discreetly removes the cover – turning it into a terrifying ceremonial.*

SIR TOBY: Come on, to't!

CESARIO, *having had some fencing practice is not bad.* SIR ANDREW, *fighting for his life, is wildly aggressive. The fight is full of ridiculous incident – ducking and weaving amongst trees, blades stuck in branches or trunks, apples falling on heads,* SIR ANDREW *dropping his sword, bending to retrieve it and being kicked by a maddened* CESARIO, *and whirling violently around the referees,* SIR TOBY *and* FABIAN, *who see the whole incident is out of hand.*

115. EXT. DAY. THE ROAD.
The wagon bearing ANTONIO *passes along the road leading to* OLIVIA'*s house.* ANTONIO *seeing it is reaching its destination*

*jumps out and dusts himself as he walks by the wall surrounding
the property. He hears the sound of fighting.*

116. EXT. DAY. OLIVIA'S ESTATE. THE ORCHARD.
CESARIO *and* SIR ANDREW *are whacking each other's
swords, coming through the trees approaching the wall as*
ANTONIO *looks over the top to see what is happening.*
   In a flash, ANTONIO *clambers up and from the top of the
wall interrupts the fighters with a great yell.*

ANTONIO:
   Put up your sword.
   Everything stops. ANTONIO *jumps down – unarmed – and
   gets in-between the amazed combatants.*
ANTONIO: If this young gentleman
   Have done offence, I take the fault on me.
SIR TOBY: You, sir! Why, what are you?
   ANTONIO *grabs* CESARIO's *sword and, confident that it is*
   SEBASTIAN *he is protecting, prepares to take on* SIR TOBY.
ANTONIO:
   One, sir, that for his love dares yet do more
   Than you have heard him brag to you he will.
SIR TOBY: Nay, if you be an undertaker, I am for you.
   *As they measure each other up with introductory fencing
   passes, there is the sound of horses and gunshots.* FABIAN
   turns in alarm.

117. EXT. DAY. OLIVIA'S ESTATE. ORCHARD ENTRANCE.
FABIAN *sees a posse of soldiers who have come in search of*
ANTONIO.

FABIAN: Sir Toby, hold! Here come the officers.

118. EXT. DAY. OLIVIA'S ESTATE. ORCHARD.
Very quickly the soldiers are everywhere, riding through the gate, leaping the wall, guns drawn, shots being fired in the air.

The two fighters make themselves scarce but ANTONIO *is too confused to escape, caught red-handed with a sword.*

SIR TOBY: I'll be with you anon.

SIR ANDREW *and* CESARIO *have hidden behind the same tree. They whisper together.*

CESARIO: Pray, sir, put your sword up.

SIR ANDREW: For that I promised you, I'll be as good as my word. He will bear you easily, and reins well.

CESARIO *ponders this double dutch but no light of understanding dawns. The soldiers manacle* ANTONIO.

SECOND OFFICER:
Antonio, I arrest thee in the name
Of Count Orsino.

ANTONIO: You do mistake me, sir.

FIRST OFFICER:
No, sir, no jot. I know your favour well,
Though now you have no sea-cap on your head.
Take him away; he knows I know him well.

ANTONIO:
I must obey.
He then steps towards CESARIO's *tree and begins addressing* CESARIO, *who immediately thinks he must be talking to* SIR ANDREW *and steps aside.*

ANTONIO (*contd*): This comes with seeking you.
What will you do, now my necessity
Makes me to ask you for my purse?

SECOND OFFICER: Come away, sir!

ANTONIO: I must entreat of you some of that money.

CESARIO *smiles in embarrassment when* ANTONIO *insists he is talking to her, and then goes closer to him to offer him some money as privately as possible.*

CESARIO:

What money, sir?

For the fair kindness you have showed me here,

Out of my lean and low ability,

I'll lend you something.

ANTONIO: Will you deny me now?

ANTONIO *dashes the coins to the ground, and is restrained in his violence by the soldiers who treat him to kicks and cuffs.*

ANTONIO (*contd*):

Is't possible that my deserts to you

Can lack persuasion!

CESARIO *shouts at him in distress, as the soldiers drag* ANTONIO *away towards the house.*

CESARIO: I know of none.

ANTONIO:

O heavens themselves!

SECOND OFFICER: Come, sir, I pray you go.

ANTONIO, *half hidden by trees, shouts back his rebuke at* CESARIO *and then is hauled away towards the out-buildings.*

ANTONIO:

This youth that you see here

I snatched one half out of the jaws of death;

Relieved him with such sanctity of love.

FIRST OFFICER:

What's that to us? To the house nearby. Away!

Go, tell my lord Orsino. We will hold him here.

Two soldiers ride off back to ORSINO'*s castle to bear the message that Illyria's public enemy number one has been captured.*

ANTONIO:

Lead me on.

*As the soldiers, some on horseback, disappear with their
prisoner,* CESARIO *leans back against a tree, almost
fainting.*

SIR TOBY *and* FABIAN *have obviously been working on*
SIR ANDREW *who is sitting on a rustic bench a bit like an
exhausted prize-fighter between rounds.*

SIR TOBY: A very dishonest, paltry boy, and more a coward
than a hare. His dishonesty appears in leaving his friend
here in necessity and denying him.

CESARIO:
Methinks his words do from such passion fly
That he believes himself; so do not I?
The others watch as CESARIO *runs off towards the house.*

FABIAN: A coward, a most devout coward, religious in it!
Suddenly, SIR ANDREW *jumps up, resolved and heads off in
pursuit of* CESARIO.

SIR ANDREW: 'Slid! I'll after him again and beat him.
SIR TOBY and FABIAN go loping after him.

SIR TOBY: Do, cuff him soundly, but never draw thy sword.

SIR ANDREW: An I do not –

119. EXT. DAY. OLIVIA'S ESTATE. OUTHOUSES.
*From a deserted and neglected set of outbuildings some distance
from the house comes a persistent banging.*

120. INT. DAY. OLIVIA'S ESTATE. THE COALSHED AMONG
THE OUTHOUSES.
The silhouetted figure of MALVOLIO *shouts through some
boarded slats.*

MALVOLIO: They have laid me here in darkness! The world
shall know it!

121. INT. DAY. OLIVIA'S HOUSE. BEDROOM.

OLIVIA *hears whistling and going to look from her bedroom
window, she sees what seems to be* CESARIO *standing by the
church with* FESTE. OLIVIA *goes delightedly to the door.*

122. EXT. DAY. OLIVIA'S ESTATE. CHURCH.

It is SEBASTIAN *who is looking at the church, in the grounds,
still using his Baedeker, and* FESTE *is still with him.*

FESTE: No, I do not know you; nor I am not sent to you by
my lady; nor your name is not Master Cesario; nor this is
not my nose, neither. Nothing that is so, is so.

SEBASTIAN: I prithee, foolish Greek, vent thy folly somewhere else; thou knowest not me.

SEBASTIAN *walks down the steps of the church to the lawn
beside* OLIVIA'S *house as* FESTE *continues to plague him.*

FESTE: Vent my folly! Tell me what I shall vent to my lady?
Shall I vent to her that thou art coming?

SEBASTIAN *is getting temperamental but can't resist playing
the coin trick on* FESTE.

SEBASTIAN: There's money for thee; if you tarry longer, I
shall give worse payment.

FESTE *has been caught on this sleight of hand before, but still
is happy to be given such a big bribe.*

FESTE: By my troth, thou hast an open hand!

SIR ANDREW, *followed by* SIR TOBY *and* FABIAN, *comes
striding from the direction of the orchard to behind*
SEBASTIAN; *he pulls him round to face him.*

SIR ANDREW: Now, sir, have I met you again? There's for
you!

SIR ANDREW *attempts a knock-out round-house punch.*
SEBASTIAN *is shaken but stands his ground, and then
unleashes a series of tremendous counter punches that whirl*

SIR ANDREW *backwards until he falls down the bank behind him.*

SEBASTIAN: Why, there's for thee! And there! And there!

He takes his coat off and throws it down, preparing to fight again, to the amazement of SIR TOBY *and* FABIAN.

SEBASTIAN: Are all the people mad?

SIR TOBY: Hold, sir, or I'll throw your dagger o'er the house.

FESTE *glances in anxiety up to the house.*

FESTE: I would not be in some of your coats, for twopence.

SIR TOBY *grabs* SEBASTIAN *as* SIR ANDREW *comes staggering to his feet.* SIR TOBY *and* SEBASTIAN *struggle.*

SIR TOBY: Come on, sir, hold!

SIR ANDREW (*threatening this previously mild boy*):
I'll have an action of battery against him, – though I struck him first, yet it's no matter for that.

SEBASTIAN: Let go thy hand!

SIR TOBY: I will not let you go, my young soldier.

SEBASTIAN:
I will be free from thee!

He breaks free, hurling a stupified SIR TOBY *to the ground and snatches up* SIR ANDREW's *sword that has been dropped.*

SEBASTIAN: What wouldst thou now?

SIR TOBY: What, what! Nay, then, I must have an ounce or two of this malapert blood from you.

*SIR TOBY *gets up, collects* CESARIO's *sword from* FABIAN *and starts to fence with* SEBASTIAN *across the lawn. There is a terrible scream.*

Running from the house comes OLIVIA *in a stricken state pushing* SEBASTIAN *back, clasping him tightly, and then turning to present her body as a barrier to protect him. She yells at* SIR TOBY.

103

OLIVIA:

Hold, Toby! On thy life, I charge thee hold!

SIR TOBY: Madam!

OLIVIA:

Will it be ever thus? Ungracious wretch,
Fit for the mountains and the barbarous caves
Where manners ne'er were preached, out of my sight!
Be not offended, dear Cesario.

While hugging and caressing SEBASTIAN *who is trying to
speak, she turns even more angrily on* SIR ANDREW.

OLIVIA:

Rudesby, be gone!

As the humiliated trio leave, OLIVIA *begins kissing*
SEBASTIAN'*s cheek and pulling him towards the terrace.*

OLIVIA: I prithee, gentle friend,
Go with me to the house,
And hear thou there how many fruitless pranks
This ruffian hath botched up, that thou thereby
Mayst smile at this. Thou shall not choose but go;
Do not deny.

SEBASTIAN *speechless with confusion breaks away to go to
pick up his coat and murmurs to himself.*

SEBASTIAN:

What relish is in this? How runs the stream?
Or I am mad, or else this is a dream.
Let fancy still my sense in Lethe steep;
If it be thus to dream, still let me sleep!

OLIVIA:

Nay, come, I prithee. Would thou'dst be ruled by me!

SEBASTIAN, *entranced by this passionate, demanding girl,
gives in.*

SEBASTIAN:

Madam, I will.

OLIVIA: O, say so, and so be!

OLIVIA *clasps him again, all caution gone, kisses him and drags him into the house past a thoughtful* FESTE.

123. EXT. DAY. THE BEACH AND DUNES.
CESARIO *is sitting overlooking the beach staring out to sea, trying to make sense of* ANTONIO's *angry outburst.*

CESARIO (*V/O*):
Prove true, imagination, oh prove true.
Her eyes are brimful of tears. She looks up and sees in the distance ORSINO, *ten or twelve soldiers and some others of his household riding towards* OLIVIA's *house. She scrambles to her feet.*

124. EXT. DAY. OLIVIA'S ESTATE. OUTHOUSES.
A grille opens with a screech and throws a pale shaft of light on to the figure of MALVOLIO, *sitting on a pile of coal, and blackened by the dust.* MALVOLIO *stirs, blinks and tries to get up. The grille slams shut.*

    MARIA, *quite disturbed and tight-lipped, turns to* FESTE *who is approaching along a rutted track, overgrown with nettles and dandelions.*

MARIA: Nay, I prithee, put on this gown and this beard; make him believe thou are Sir Topas the curate.
    MARIA *goes away looking for* SIR TOBY.
FESTE: I would I were the first that ever dissembled in such a gown.
    SIR TOBY *arrives with* MARIA *very obviously drunk, and carrying a bottle of Scotch whisky half-consumed.*
SIR TOBY: God bless thee, Master Parson!
FESTE: *Bonos dies*, Sir Toby; for as the old hermit of Prague that never saw pen and ink very wittily said to a niece of King Gorboduc: that that is, is. So I being Master Parson,

106

am Master Parson; for what is 'that' but 'that'? and 'is' but 'is'?

SIR TOBY *recognizes* FESTE *and during the gobbledygook satire of the real parson, he sits on a wood chopping block close to the doorway, puts down his bottle, and takes a glass from one pocket and biscuits out of the other, preparing to enjoy the show.*

SIR TOBY: To him, Master Topas.

FESTE, *fully disguised in beard, hat and cassock, bangs on the grille and after a while opens it.*

FESTE: What ho, I say! Peace in this prison!

MALVOLIO *comes up as close to the grille as he can, stumbling and quivering. His face is both blackened and bruised.*

MALVOLIO: Who calls there?

FESTE: Master Topas the curate, who comes to visit Malvolio the lunatic.

MALVOLIO: Master Topas, Master Topas, good Master Topas, go to my lady –

FESTE *moves past the grille, sometimes staying out of* MALVOLIO's *line of vision and sometimes looking in.*

FESTE: Out, hyperbolical fiend! Talkest thou nothing but of ladies?

SIR TOBY *drinks and eats.*

SIR TOBY (*to* MARIA): The knave counterfeits well.

MALVOLIO: Good Master Topas, do not think I am mad. They have laid me here in hideous darkness –

FESTE: Sayst thou that this house is dark?

MALVOLIO: As hell, Master Topas.

FESTE: Why, it hath bay windows transparent as barricadoes, and the clerestories toward the south-north are as lustrous as ebony.

MALVOLIO: I am not mad. I say to you, this house is dark.

FESTE: Madman, thou errest. I say there is no darkness but ignorance.

MALVOLIO: I am no more mad than you are – make the trial of it in any constant question.

MALVOLIO is looking out. FESTE's bearded head is in grim and alarming silhouette.

FESTE: What is the opinion of Pythagoras concerning wildfowl?

MALVOLIO: That the soul of our grandam might haply inhabit a bird.

FESTE: What thinkest thou of his opinion?

MALVOLIO: I think nobly of the soul, and no way approve his opinion.

FESTE: Thou shalt hold the opinion of Pythagoras ere I will allow of thy wits, and fear to kill a woodcock lest thou dispossess the soul of thy grandam. Fare thee well.

Suddenly the grille smashes shut plunging everything into darkness. MALVOLIO goes on yelling in the dark.

125. INT. DAY. OLIVIA'S HOUSE. DRAWING-ROOM.
SEBASTIAN and OLIVIA are locked in a passionate embrace, lying together full-length on the sofa of the drawing-room. OLIVIA breaks and gets up, breathless, laughing and urging SEBASTIAN, who is following her, to stay put; she goes backwards to the french windows and out on to the terrace. SEBASTIAN stands in the open doorway after OLIVIA has gone.

SEBASTIAN:

    This is the air; that is the glorious sun;
    This pearl she gave me, I do feel't and see't.
    He goes to look at himself in the large wall mirror, and conducts a self-questioning dialogue, like twins conversing.
SEBASTIAN:

    Yet doth this accident and flood of fortune

So far exceed all instance, all discourse,
That I am ready to distrust mine eyes,
And wrangle with my reason that persuades me
To any other trust but that I am mad –

126. EXT. DAY. OLIVIA'S ESTATE. OUTHOUSES.

MALVOLIO (*shouting*): I am not mad!
   SIR TOBY *finishes another drink, and eats the last biscuit.*
   MARIA *looks distressed and pained.*
SIR TOBY: I would we were well rid of this knavery.
   He shakes FESTE *grimly and unsteadily by the hand, as*
   MALVOLIO *whimpers and cries out behind the door. The*
   revenge is cruelly satisfied.
SIR TOBY: For I am now so far in offence with my niece that
   I cannot pursue't with any safety.
   SIR TOBY *goes a few paces and turns.* MARIA *goes to*
   support him. SIR TOBY *grabs her and kisses her fiercely on*
   the mouth and the throat, aroused by the whole incident.
SIR TOBY (*to* MARIA): Come by and by to my chamber.
   SIR TOBY *lurches away.* MARIA *adjusts herself and looks*
   clandestinely at FESTE *who is shaking his head slowly at her.*
   MARIA *breathes deeply, and then goes with whatever dignity*
   she can retain.
      FESTE *divests himself of robe and beard while singing*
   recognizably as himself.
FESTE (*sings*):
      Hey Robin, jolly Robin!
      Tell me how thy lady does –
MALVOLIO (*V/O*): Feste! Feste!
FESTE (*sings*):
      My lady is unkind, perdy.
      Who calls, ha?

MALVOLIO (*V/O*): Good Feste, help me to a candle, and
pen, ink, and paper.

FESTE *pulls open the grille and looks in.*

FESTE:

Master Malvolio?

Alas, sir, how fell you besides your five wits?

MALVOLIO *comes blinded towards the light, stumbling and
sobbing.*

MALVOLIO: There was never man so notoriously abused.
They have here propertied me; keep me in darkness, send
ministers to me – asses!

FESTE: Advise you what you say. The minister is here.
*He suddenly ducks away in a show of mock innocence. He
ducks back under the grille to the side he was just on and
becomes 'the priest' again.*

FESTE (*in priest's voice*): Malvolio, Malvolio, thy wits the
heavens restore! Endeavour thyself to sleep and leave thy
vain bibble-babble.

MALVOLIO: Master Topas!

FESTE *continues to dive between the two places in
conversation with himself.*

FESTE (*in priest's voice*): Maintain no words with him, good
fellow. (*In own voice.*) Who, I sir? Not I, sir! God bye you,
good Master Topas! (*In priest's voice.*) Marry, amen! (*In
own voice.*) I will, sir, I will.

MALVOLIO *follows the talk with his eyes, afraid of the
priest's displeasure. He listens and risking that the priest has
gone, he whispers.*

MALVOLIO: Feste, Feste, I say!

FESTE *reappears at the window grille.*

FESTE: Alas, sir, be patient. I am shent for speaking to you.

MALVOLIO: I tell thee, I am as well in my wits as any man
in Illyria.

FESTE: Well-a-day, that you were, sir!

110

MALVOLIO: By this hand, I am! Good Feste, some ink, paper, and light; and convey what I will set down to my lady.

127. EXT. DAY. OLIVIA'S HOUSE. THE GARDEN AND CHURCH. SEBASTIAN *looks around over the house, the estate and the church across the lawn, as he walks and turns. We see his POV, revolving around* OLIVIA's *beautiful domain.*

SEBASTIAN:
Or else the lady's mad; yet if 'twere so,
She should not sway her house, command her followers,
Take and give back affairs and their dispatch,
With such a smooth, discreet, and stable bearing
As I perceive she does. There's something in't
That is deceivable.
OLIVIA *emerges from the church tugging a cassocked* PRIEST *along behind her, a bearded man who it is clear* FESTE *had been impersonating.* OLIVIA *rushes up to* SEBASTIAN *and they meet on the lawn, as she makes her breathless proposal, striking while the iron is hot.*

OLIVIA:
Blame not this haste of mine. If you mean well,
Now go with me and with this holy man
Into the chantry by; there before him
Plight me the full assurance of your faith,
That my most jealous and too doubtful soul
May live at peace. He shall conceal it
Whiles you are willing it shall come to note;
What do you say?
SEBASTIAN *is in irresistable wonderland.*

SEBASTIAN:
I'll follow this good man, and go with you;
And having sworn truth, ever will be true.

111

OLIVIA *tugs* SEBASTIAN *towards the church. The* PRIEST
*is dumbfounded, and turns to follow them back into the
church.*

128. EXT. DAY. OLIVIA'S ESTATE. OUTHOUSES.

FESTE: But tell me true, are you not mad indeed, or do you
but counterfeit?

MALVOLIO: Believe me, I am not. I tell thee true.

FESTE *presses his face right into the bars, distorting his
features.*

FESTE: Nay, I'll ne'er believe a madman till I see his brains.
I will fetch you light, and paper, and ink.

FESTE *slams shut the shutter and crossing the yard, calls out.*

FESTE (*sings*):
   I am gone, sir, and anon, sir,
      I'll be with you again.

129. EXT. DAY. OLIVIA'S ESTATE. CHURCH.

FESTE *is approaching the church in which candles are burning.*
OLIVIA *and* SEBASTIAN *emerge followed by the* PRIEST.
FESTE *half hides and watches the newly-married couple kiss.
He murmurs to himself.*

FESTE (*sings*):
   In a trice, like to the old vice,
      Your need to sustain.
   Who with dagger of lath, in his rage and his wrath
      Cries 'Ah ha!' to the devil.

FESTE *climbs up on a piece of masonry and peers through a
church window.*

130. INT. DAY. OLIVIA'S ESTATE. CHURCH.

Through the glass, FESTE *sees* MARIA *led by a grim, unsteady* SIR TOBY *move nervously towards the altar rail as the* PRIEST *returns questioningly towards them.*

FESTE (*sings*):
Like a mad lad – 'Pare thy nails, dad?
Adieu, goodman, devil!'

131. EXT. DAY. OLIVIA'S ESTATE. STABLES AND COURTYARD.

ORSINO *rides with* CURIO *and* VALENTINE *and other servants into the stables area of* OLIVIA'*s house, with* CESARIO *clinging on behind* ORSINO. *The soldiers and officers springing to action yell instructions and open the stable door in which* ANTONIO *is being held prisoner.* ORSINO *and* CESARIO *dismount.* FESTE *scuttles through the stable-yard followed importunately by* FABIAN, *nervous that the letter from* MALVOLIO *will incriminate him.*

FABIAN: Now, as thou lov'st me, let me see his letter.
ORSINO *sees them and turns away from the business of* ANTONIO *to give what he takes to be* OLIVIA'*s servants a message for* OLIVIA.
ORSINO: Belong you to the Lady Olivia, friends?
FESTE: Ay, sir, we are some of her trappings.
ORSINO (*warily*): I know thee well. How dost thou, my good fellow?
FESTE: Truly, sir, the better for my foes, and the worse for my friends. They praise me – and make an ass of me. Now my foes tell me plainly, I am an ass; so that by my foes, sir, I profit in the knowledge of myself, and by my friends I am abused.
ORSINO: Why, this is excellent.
ORSINO *gives* FESTE *a coin.*

FESTE: By my troth, sir, no – though it please you to be one of my friends.

ORSINO *is patient in the face of* FESTE's *mischief.*

ORSINO: If you will let your lady know I am here, and bring her along with you, it may awake my bounty further.

FESTE: Marry, sir, lullaby to your bounty till I come again.

ORSINO *goes back towards the soldiers as* ANTONIO *is dragged into the light and stares in contempt at* CESARIO.

CESARIO: This is the man, sir, that did rescue me.

ORSINO's *manner changes and he becomes every inch the soldier prince.*

ORSINO:

That face of his I do remember well.

Yet when I saw it last, it was besmeared

As black as Vulcan in the smoke of war.

FIRST OFFICER:

Orsino, this is that Antonio

That took the *Phoenix*, he that did the *Tiger* board

When your young cousin Titus lost his leg.

CESARIO *is anxious to appease.*

CESARIO:

He did me kindness, sir, drew on my side.

ORSINO *walks up to face* ANTONIO.

ORSINO:

Notable pirate, thou salt-water thief,

What foolish boldness brought thee to their mercies

Whom thou, in terms so bloody and so dear,

Hast made thine enemies?

ANTONIO:

Orsino, noble sir,

Antonio never yet was thief or pirate;

Though, I confess, on base and ground enough,

Orsino's enemy. A witchcraft drew me hither.

That most ingrateful boy there by your side.

CESARIO *looks incredulous and angry by turns.*

114

ANTONIO (*in furious contempt*):
  His life I gave him, and did thereto add
  My love without retention. For his sake
  Faced the danger of this adverse town.
  The toughest of men, ANTONIO, *becomes choked with distress.*
CESARIO:
  How can this be?
ORSINO: When came he to this town?
ANTONIO:
  Yesterday; and for three months before
  Both day and night, did we keep company.

132. EXT. DAY. OLIVIA'S GARDEN.
OLIVIA *emerges from her house, followed by two of the maids
from the household who bring trays of hock in long stemmed
glasses and four men servants who bring mugs of beer for the
soldiers.*

ORSINO:
  Here comes the Countess; now heaven walks on earth!
  But for thee, fellow – fellow, thy words are madness.
  Three months this youth hath tended upon me.
  ORSINO *leads his group up towards the lawn, followed by a
  bemused* ANTONIO *under guard.* ORSINO *accepts the
  proffered wine and drinks a ceremonial greeting to* OLIVIA.
OLIVIA:
  What would my lord – but that he may not have –
  Cesario, you do not keep promise with me.
CESARIO (*horrified*):
  Madam?
ORSINO:
  Gracious Olivia –
OLIVIA: What do you say, Cesario?
  (*Impatiently to* ORSINO.)
  Good, my lord.

CESARIO *stays resolutely behind* ORSINO, *grimacing facial signals at* OLIVIA.

CESARIO:

My lord would speak; my duty hushes me.

OLIVIA:

If it be aught to the old tune, my lord,
It is as fat and fulsome to mine ear
As howling after music.

ORSINO:

Still so cruel?

OLIVIA: Still so constant, lord.
The pleasant social scene is turning ugly.

ORSINO:

What, to perverseness? You uncivil lady,
My soul the faithfull'st offerings hath breathed out
That e'er devotion tendered! What shall I do?
ORSINO *throws his wine away and the glass smashes against a garden urn.*

OLIVIA:

Even what it please my lord, that shall become him.

ORSINO:

Why should I not – in savage jealousy
Like to th'Egyptian thief at point of death
Kill what I love? But, madam, hear me this:
Since you to non-regardance cast my faith,
And that I partly know the instrument
That screws me from my true place in your favour,
Live you the marble-breasted tyrant still.
He clasps CESARIO's *hand again.*

ORSINO:

But this your minion, whom I know you love,
And whom, by heaven, I swear, I tender dearly,
Him will I tear out of that cruel eye.

CESARIO:

And I, most jocund, apt, and willingly
116

To do you rest, a thousand deaths would die.

ORSINO:

Come, boy, with me, my thoughts are ripe in mischief.

OLIVIA goes to break the clasp, in passionate defence of her
man. The tussle becomes a tug of war, unseemly and shocking.

OLIVIA:

Where goes Cesario?

CESARIO: After him I love

More than I love these eyes, more than my life,
More by all mores than e'er I shall love wife.

ORSINO and CESARIO begin to leave through the crowd of
drinkers.

OLIVIA:

Ay me, detested! How am I beguiled!

CESARIO returns in exasperation to confront OLIVIA.

CESARIO:

Who does beguile you? Who does do you wrong?

OLIVIA:

Hast thou forgot thyself? Is it so long?
Call forth the holy father!

Two of the men servants run off – one to the house, the other
over the lawns to the church – but CESARIO goes back to
leave with ORSINO.

ORSINO: Come away!

ORSINO is heading with CESARIO for the stables.

OLIVIA:

Whither, my lord? Cesario, husband, stay!

CESARIO stops. ORSINO stops and turns first to OLIVIA.

ORSINO:

Husband?

OLIVIA: Ay, husband. Can he that deny?

ORSINO (*to CESARIO*):

Her husband, sirrah?

CESARIO: No, my lord, not I.

OLIVIA *runs after* CESARIO, *hugs her and tries to make an embrace.*

OLIVIA:

Fear not, Cesario, take thy fortunes up.
She breaks off and runs towards the PRIEST *who is being brought from the house.*

OLIVIA:

O, welcome, Father.
Father, I charge thee, by thy reverence,
Here to unfold – though lately we intended
To keep in darkness – what thou dost know
Hath newly passed between this youth and me.

PRIEST:

A contract of eternal bond of love,
Confirmed by mutual joinder of your hands,
Strengthened by interchangement of your rings,
Sealed in my function, by my testimony.
ORSINO *turns to* CESARIO, *suddenly winded, almost losing his voice. He takes a surprisingly intimate farewell of his betrayer.*

ORSINO:

O thou dissembling cub! What wilt thou be
When time hath sowed a grizzle on thy case?
Farewell, and take her; but direct thy feet
Where thou and I henceforth may never meet.

CESARIO:

My lord, I do protest –
Again OLIVIA *clasps* CESARIO *as* ORSINO *walks unsteadily away.*

OLIVIA: O, do not swear!
Hold little faith, though thou hast too much fear.
SIR ANDREW *appears running from the main entrance of the house. He bellows across the lawn.*

SIR ANDREW: For the love of God, a surgeon! Send one presently to Sir Toby!

118

People begin to run towards the house imagining some death dealing disaster.

OLIVIA: What's the matter?

OLIVIA leads ORSINO and CESARIO at full pelt towards the new crisis.

SIR ANDREW (*tearfully*): He's broke my head across, and he's given Sir Toby a bloody coxcomb too. For the love of God, your help! I had rather than forty pounds I were at home.

OLIVIA: Who has done this, Sir Andrew?

SIR ANDREW: The Count's gentleman, one Cesario. He's the very devil incardinate.

ORSINO: My gentleman, Cesario?

SIR ANDREW realizes first of all that he is addressing the Duke, before recoiling at the sight of CESARIO.

SIR ANDREW: 'Od's lifelings, here he is! (*Coming towards CESARIO.*) You broke my head for nothing; and that I did, I was set on to do't by Sir Toby.

CESARIO:
Why do you speak to me? I never hurt you.
You drew your sword upon me without cause.

SIR ANDREW: If a bloody coxcomb be a hurt, you have hurt me.

SIR TOBY helped by FESTE comes out of the house and slumps by a little fountain in the middle of the lawn.

SIR ANDREW: Here comes Sir Toby halting; but if he had not been in drink, he would have tickled you othergates than he did.

FESTE bathes the blood away from SIR TOBY's forehead and neck.

ORSINO *steps up to them to take some control of a wildly deteriorating situation.*

ORSINO: How now, gentlemen? How is't with you?

SIR TOBY: That's all one; he's hurt me, and there's the end on't. (*Wincing, to* FESTE.) Sot, didst see Dick Surgeon, sot?

FESTE: O, he's drunk, Sir Toby, an hour agone.

MARIA *runs from the house in ill-disguised panic, as* SIR TOBY *quietly recognizes a truth.*

SIR TOBY: I hate a drunken rogue.

OLIVIA *urges* MARIA *to take* SIR TOBY *round to the back of the house — to the servants' area.*

OLIVIA: Away with him! Who hath made this havoc with them?

SIR ANDREW: I'll help you, Sir Toby, because we'll be dressed together.

SIR TOBY *roughly pushes* SIR ANDREW *away, to the point where* SIR ANDREW *staggers back.*

SIR TOBY: Will you help? An asshead, and a coxcomb, and a knave — a thin-faced knave, a gull!

SIR TOBY *fleers at him and then laughs at the shocked spectators. He refuses help and walks unsteadily with* MARIA *and the servants away towards a side door of the house.*

OLIVIA *goes to* SIR ANDREW *who is standing ashen and still.*

OLIVIA: Get him to bed, and let his hurt be looked to.

He stares at her, very gently kisses her hand and with painful dignity, walks away in the opposite direction from SIR TOBY. CESARIO *goes after him to make peace but gives up.*

Across the lawn the other way comes SEBASTIAN, *running through the assorted bystanders.*

SEBASTIAN:
I am sorry, madam, I have hurt your kinsman.
But had it been the brother of my blood
I must have done no less, with wit and safety.
Pardon me, sweet one, even for the vows

121

We made each other but so late ago.

He kisses OLIVIA *looks around the different faces agape at his appearance, nods to* ORSINO *and then rushes to embrace* ANTONIO, *who is, with his guards, the most distant figure.*

SEBASTIAN:

Antonio! O, my dear Antonio!

How have the hours racked and tortured me

Since I have lost thee!

ANTONIO:

Sebastian, are you?

SEBASTIAN: Fear'st thou that, Antonio?

ANTONIO:

How have you made division of yourself?

He looks over SEBASTIAN'*s shoulder at* CESARIO *who is standing, framed only by trees, looking in the direction of the departing* SIR ANDREW.

ANTONIO:

Which is Sebastian?

OLIVIA *looks first at* SEBASTIAN *and then at* CESARIO.

OLIVIA: Most wonderful!

CESARIO *turns and sees her drowned brother.* SEBASTIAN *sees a mirror image of himself.* CESARIO *begins very slowly to walk towards this apparition. As if drawn to behave like a mirror image,* SEBASTIAN *walks towards the other boy.*

SEBASTIAN:

Do I stand there? I never had a brother;

I had a sister

Whom the blind waves and surges have devoured.

Of charity, what kin are you to me?

What countryman? What name? What parentage?

CESARIO:

Of Messaline. Sebastian was my father.

Such a Sebastian was my brother too.

So went he suited to his watery tomb.

122

SEBASTIAN:

    Were you a woman, as the rest goes even,
    I should my tears let fall upon your cheek,
    And say, 'Thrice welcome, drownèd Viola.'
    They stop, close to each other.

CESARIO:

    My father had a mole upon his brow.

SEBASTIAN:

    And so had mine.

CESARIO:

    And died that day when Viola from her birth ...

SEBASTIAN:

    That day that made my sister thirteen years.

CESARIO:

    If nothing lets to make us happy both
    But this my masculine usurped attire,
    Do not embrace me, till each circumstance
    Of place, time, fortune, do cohere and jump
    That I am ...

    SEBASTIAN *reaches out his hand and with the same
    precision as before he takes the end of the moustache and
    peels it off.*

CESARIO: ... Viola.

    *The twins touch hands, touch each other's faces, touch each
    other's tears.*

VIOLA: Which to confirm,
    I'll bring you to a captain; by whose help
    I was preserved to serve this noble Count.

    OLIVIA *is beginning to understand the meaning all this gives
    to her many desperate pleadings with* CESARIO. *She is
    giving way to embarrassment when* SEBASTIAN *kisses her on
    the lips.*

SEBASTIAN:

    So comes it, lady, you have been mistook.
    But nature to her bias drew in that.

You would have been contracted to a maid.
Nor are you therein, by my life, deceived:
You are betrothed both to a maid and man.

ORSINO smiles at OLIVIA and then at SEBASTIAN, whose hand he shakes.

ORSINO:
If this be so, as yet the glass seems true,
I shall have share in this most happy wrack.

He goes to VIOLA who cannot hold his gaze and turns her back. He whispers to the back of VIOLA's head.

ORSINO:
Boy, thou hast said to me a thousand times
Thou never shouldst love woman like to me.

She shakes her head, but murmurs her vow, unable to look at the man she has deceived.

VIOLA:
And all those sayings will I overswear
And all those swearings keep as true in soul
As doth that orbèd continent the fire
That severs day from night.

ORSINO: Give me thy hand.
Your master quits you; and for your service done him
So much against the mettle of your sex,
Here is my hand; you shall from this time be
Your master's mistress.

ORSINO turns VIOLA around, clasps her hand as he has done before, and then passionately kisses her. The man is kissing the boy who is now revealed as the girl.

ORSINO:
And let me see thee in thy woman's weeds.

ORSINO and VIOLA laugh spontaneously at the thought of what has occurred between them since they met.

ANTONIO watches full of feeling, and then lowers his eyes, realizing he alone does not partake of this resolution.

ORSINO *goes to* ANTONIO *and the manacles binding his hands are released. He brings* ANTONIO *to* SEBASTIAN *who takes him to* VIOLA. *Then* SEBASTIAN *and* VIOLA *hug again as* ANTONIO *laughs. Finally* OLIVIA *and* VIOLA *come face to face. It is a difficult moment.* OLIVIA *overcomes her tears and reaches out her hands to* VIOLA. *They embrace.*

OLIVIA:

A sister, you are she.

FESTE *steps forward to* VIOLA *and pulls from his coat pocket the necklace — discarded by* VIOLA *on the beach when first she was cast up by the storm.* FESTE *puts it around her neck. She looks wonderingly at him. He turns and takes a letter from his other pocket and goes to* OLIVIA. FESTE *holds up the back of the letter for* OLIVIA *to read.*

OLIVIA: From Malvolio?

133. INT. DAY. OLIVIA'S HOUSE. HALL.
The hall is full of servants, on the stairs and looking over the galleried landings. They begin to applaud because the news has reached them that their mistress is married and another betrothal has taken place. The applause suddenly breaks down and stops.

MALVOLIO, *coal-blackened, clothes ripped, garters hanging and dragging behind him and without his toupee to cover his receding grey hair, has arrived in the hall which was his domain.*

OLIVIA:

How now, Malvolio?

MALVOLIO:

Madam, you have done me wrong;
Notorious wrong.

OLIVIA: Have I, Malvolio? No!

MALVOLIO:

Lady, you have; pray you, peruse that letter.
You must not now deny it is your hand.

126

158

Write from it if you can, in hand or phrase,
Or say 'tis not your seal, not your invention;
You can say none of this. Well, grant it then,
And tell me in the modesty of honour,
Why you have given me such clear lights of favour?
Bade me come smiling and cross-gartered to you,
To put on yellow stockings, and to frown
Upon Sir Toby and the lighter people?
*Whispers and sniggers of laughter become audible amongst
the maids and servants above.*

MALVOLIO:

And, acting this in an obedient hope,
Why have you suffered me to be imprisoned,
Kept in a dark house, visited by the priest,
And made the most notorious geck and gull
That e'er invention played on? Tell me why?

OLIVIA:

Alas, Malvolio, this is not my writing,
Though, I confess, much like the character.
MALVOLIO *is caught in a rictus of appalled contemplation
as* OLIVIA *goes to the desk in the hall and takes out some of
her own writing.*

OLIVIA:

But out of question 'tis Maria's hand.
She goes up to MALVOLIO *and takes his feelingless hand.
She talks very quietly to him, trying to save him from more
ignominy.*

OLIVIA:

This practice hath most shrewdly passed upon thee;
But when we know the grounds and authors of it,
Thou shalt be both the plaintiff and the judge
Of thine own cause.
FABIAN, *backed by several other servants, speaks from the
other side of the hall.*

128

FABIAN: Good madam, hear me speak;
Most freely I confess; Maria writ
The letter at Sir Toby's great importance,
In recompense whereof, he hath married her.
*The servants on the stairs and in the hall respond in disbelief
and amused shock.*

OLIVIA:
Alas, poor fool! How have they baffled thee!
FABIAN *tries to be a peacemaker, urging all the other
servants and the assembled masters and mistresses to forgive
and forget.*

FABIAN:
But let no quarrel, nor no brawl to come,
Taint the condition of this present hour,
Which I have wondered at.
But, FESTE *is now at the first gallery level looking down.*

FESTE (*publicly*): Why, 'Some are born great, some achieve
greatness, and some have greatness thrown upon them.'
*He descends, passing all those congregated, to the floor level,
where everyone can see he is wearing* MALVOLIO's *toupee.*

FESTE: I was one, sir, in this interlude, one Master Topas,
sir. 'By the Lord, fool, I am not mad!' But do you
remember: 'Madam, why laugh you at such a barren
rascal?'
He thrusts his face into MALVOLIO's *face, now twisted in
misery.*

FESTE: And you smile not, he's gagged? And thus the
whirligig of time brings in his revenges.
He hands MALVOLIO's *toupee, his disguise, back to its
shamed owner and walks away through the crowd and out of
sight.*

   MALVOLIO *looks at the lovers holding hands, and then at*
ANTONIO, *the guards, the valets, the gardeners, the maids
and his eyes harden with hatred.*

MALVOLIO:

I'll be revenged on the whole pack of you!

MALVOLIO *stumbles through the throng towards his room.*
He slumps at the door. Several of the servants go to him
involuntarily and help him towards some privacy. As
MALVOLIO *is aware of people helping him he becomes*
dignified, determined to leave without assistance.

OLIVIA:

He hath been most notoriously abused.

ORSINO *calls out to* FABIAN.

ORSINO:

Pursue him and entreat him to a peace.

He returns to VIOLA *who is holding* SEBASTIAN's *hand –*
who reaches out for OLIVIA.

ORSINO:

When that is done, and golden time convents,
A solemn combination shall be made
Of our dear souls.

134. EXT. EVENING. OLIVIA'S ESTATE. ROAD.

FESTE *begins to sing as he leaves the house.*

FESTE (*sings*):

When that I was and a little tiny boy,
    With hey-ho, the wind and the rain;

He is passed by SIR ANDREW *being driven away in a pony*
and trap, piled with luggage, the first to leave this romantic
paradise for the real world.

FESTE (*sings*):

A foolish thing was but a toy,
    For the rain it raineth every day.

135. EXT. EVENING. OLIVIA'S ESTATE. THE GATEHOUSE.

FESTE (*sings*):

> But when I came to man's estate,
>> With hey-ho, the wind and the rain;

Then as he stands by the gate, ANTONIO *emerges and strides grimly away from the house, from Illyria.*

FESTE (*sings*):

> 'Gainst knaves and thieves men shut their gate,
>> For the rain it raineth every day.

136. INT. EVENING. OLIVIA'S HOUSE. HALL.
The happy lovers hug and embrace.

ORSINO:

Meantime, sweet sister,
We will not part from hence.
Cesario, come.
For so you shall be, while you are a man.
But when in other habits you are seen –
Orsino's mistress, and his fancy's queen!

137. EXT. EVENING. OLIVIA'S ESTATE. ROAD.

FESTE (*sings*):

> But when I came, alas, to wive,
>> With hey-ho, the wind and the rain;

Then on a wayside estate road, FESTE *watches* SIR TOBY *and* MARIA, *struggling with luggage, get into an omnibus coach.* MARIA *looks back towards the house, and then at* FESTE. *She half-smiles and disappears inside the coach.*

FESTE (*sings*):

> By swaggering could I never thrive,
>> For the rain it raineth every day.

But when I came unto my beds,
  With hey-ho, the wind and the rain;

138. EXT. EVENING. OLIVIA'S ESTATE. ANOTHER ROAD.
FESTE *sees* MALVOLIO, *devoid of his butler's uniform and carrying a small suitcase, walking along the road leading out of the estate, turning his collar up against the cold.*

FESTE (*sings*):
  With tosspots still had drunken heads,
    For the rain it raineth every day.

139. INT. DAY. OLIVIA'S HOUSE. BALLROOM.
The ballroom is now thronging with people celebrating the double wedding of the lovers. VIOLA, *very much a girl again, and* OLIVIA *are sumptuously dressed in beautiful gowns; the men are men, the women are women* ... ORSINO, SEBASTIAN, OLIVIA *and* VIOLA *thread their way through a chain which conjures memories of all their previous relationships.*

140. EXT. DAY. THE CLIFFS.
FESTE *sits on the cliff top overlooking the sea where the shipwreck occurred and his story began.*

FESTE (*sings*):
  A great while ago the world began,
    With hey-ho, the wind and the rain;
  But that's all one, my tale is done,
    And I'll strive to please you every day.
He gets up, swings his tattered bag containing his worldly goods on to his shoulder and clambers down the path, to begin his next journey. He disappears from view. The sun sets and the sea washes ceaselessly on to the shore.

METHUEN SCREENPLAYS

☐ BEAUTIFUL THING	Jonathan Harvey	£6.99
☐ THE ENGLISH PATIENT	Anthony Minghella	£7.99
☐ THE CRUCIBLE	Arthur Miller	£6.99
☐ THE WIND IN THE WILLOWS	Terry Jones	£7.99
☐ PERSUASION	Jane Austen, adapted by Nick Dear	£6.99
☐ TWELFTH NIGHT	Shakespeare, adapted by Trevor Nunn	£7.99
☐ THE KRAYS	Philip Ridley	£7.99
☐ THE AMERICAN DREAMS (THE REFLECTING SKIN & THE PASSION OF DARKLY NOON)	Philip Ridley	£8.99
☐ MRS BROWN	Jeremy Brock	£7.99
☐ THE GAMBLER	Dostoyevsky, adapted by Nick Dear	£7.99
☐ TROJAN EDDIE	Billy Roche	£7.99
☐ THE WINGS OF THE DOVE	Hossein Amini	£7.99
☐ THE ACID HOUSE TRILOGY	Irvine Welsh	£8.99
☐ THE LONG GOOD FRIDAY	Barrie Keeffe	£6.99
☐ SLING BLADE	Billy Bob Thornton	£7.99

● All Methuen Drama books are available through mail order or from your local bookshop.

Please send cheque/eurocheque/postal order (sterling only) Access, Visa, Mastercard, Diners Card, Switch or Amex.

☐☐☐☐☐☐☐☐☐☐☐☐☐☐☐☐

Expiry Date:_____Signature: _____

Please allow 75 pence per book for post and packing U.K.
Overseas customers please allow £1.00 per copy for post and packing.

ALL ORDERS TO:

Methuen Books, Books by Post, TBS Limited, The Book Service, Colchester Road, Frating Green, Colchester, Essex CO7 7DW.

NAME: _____

ADDRESS: _____

_____

_____

Please allow 28 days for delivery. Please tick box if you do not
wish to receive any additional information   ☐

Prices and availability subject to change without notice.

A SELECTED LIST OF
METHUEN MODERN PLAYS

☐ CLOSER	Patrick Marber	£6.99
☐ THE BEAUTY QUEEN OF LEENANE	Martin McDonagh	£6.99
☐ A SKULL IN CONNEMARA	Martin McDonagh	£6.99
☐ THE LONESOME WEST	Martin McDonagh	£6.99
☐ THE CRIPPLE OF INISHMAAN	Martin McDonagh	£6.99
☐ THE STEWARD OF CHRISTENDOM	Sebastian Barry	£6.99
☐ SHOPPING AND F***ING	Mark Ravenhill	£6.99
☐ FAUST (FAUST IS DEAD)	Mark Ravenhill	£5.99
☐ POLYGRAPH	Robert Lepage and Marie Brassard	£6.99
☐ BEAUTIFUL THING	Jonathan Harvey	£6.99
☐ MEMORY OF WATER & FIVE KINDS OF SILENCE	Shelagh Stephenson	£7.99
☐ WISHBONES	Lucinda Coxon	£6.99
☐ BONDAGERS & THE STRAW CHAIR	Sue Glover	£9.99
☐ SOME VOICES & PALE HORSE	Joe Penhall	£7.99
☐ KNIVES IN HENS	David Harrower	£6.99
☐ BOYS' LIFE & SEARCH AND DESTROY	Howard Korder	£8.99
☐ THE LIGHTS	Howard Korder	£6.99
☐ SERVING IT UP & A WEEK WITH TONY	David Eldridge	£8.99
☐ INSIDE TRADING	Malcolm Bradbury	£6.99
☐ MASTERCLASS	Terrence McNally	£5.99
☐ EUROPE & THE ARCHITECT	David Greig	£7.99
☐ BLUE MURDER	Peter Nichols	£6.99
☐ BLASTED & PHAEDRA'S LOVE	Sarah Kane	£7.99

• All Methuen Drama books are available through mail order or from your local bookshop.

Please send cheque/eurocheque/postal order (sterling only) Access, Visa, Mastercard, Diners Card, Switch or Amex.

☐☐☐☐☐☐☐☐☐☐☐☐☐☐☐☐

Expiry Date:_____ Signature: _____

Please allow 75 pence per book for post and packing U.K.
Overseas customers please allow £1.00 per copy for post and packing.

ALL ORDERS TO:

Methuen Books, Books by Post, TBS Limited, The Book Service, Colchester Road, Frating Green, Colchester, Essex CO7 7DW.

NAME: _____

ADDRESS: _____

_____

_____

Please allow 28 days for delivery. Please tick box if you do not wish to receive any additional information ☐

Prices and availability subject to change without notice.

METHUEN DRAMA
MONOLOGUE & SCENE BOOKS

☐ CONTEMPORARY SCENES FOR ACTORS (MEN)	Earley and Keil	£8.99
☐ CONTEMPORARY SCENES FOR ACTORS (WOMEN)	Earley and Keil	£8.99
☐ THE CLASSICAL MONOLOGUE (MEN)	Earley and Keil	£7.99
☐ THE CLASSICAL MONOLOGUE (WOMEN)	Earley and Keil	£7.99
☐ THE CONTEMPORARY MONOLOGUE (MEN)	Earley and Keil	£7.99
☐ THE CONTEMPORARY MONOLOGUE (WOMEN)	Earley and Keil	£7.99
☐ THE MODERN MONOLOGUE (MEN)	Earley and Keil	£7.99
☐ THE MODERN MONOLOGUE (WOMEN)	Earley and Keil	£7.99
☐ THE METHUEN AUDITION BOOK FOR MEN	Annika Bluhm	£6.99
☐ THE METHUEN AUDITION BOOK FOR WOMEN	Annika Bluhm	£6.99
☐ THE METHUEN AUDITION BOOK FOR YOUNG ACTORS	Anne Harvey	£6.99
☐ THE METHUEN BOOK OF DUOLOGUES FOR YOUNG ACTORS	Anne Harvey	£6.99

• All Methuen Drama books are available through mail order or from your local bookshop.

Please send cheque/eurocheque/postal order (sterling only) Access, Visa, Mastercard, Diners Card, Switch or Amex.

☐☐☐☐☐☐☐☐☐☐☐☐☐☐☐☐

Expiry Date: _____ Signature: _____

Please allow 75 pence per book for post and packing U.K.
Overseas customers please allow £1.00 per copy for post and packing.

ALL ORDERS TO:

Methuen Books, Books by Post, TBS Limited, The Book Service, Colchester Road, Frating Green, Colchester, Essex CO7 7DW.

NAME: _____

ADDRESS: _____

Please allow 28 days for delivery. Please tick box if you do not wish to receive any additional information ☐

Prices and availability subject to change without notice.

Companies, institutions and other organisations wishing to make bulk
purchases of any Methuen Drama books published by Random House
should contact their local bookseller or Random House direct: Product
Manager, Methuen Drama, Random House UK Ltd, 20 Vauxhall Bridge
Road, London SW1V 2SA. Tel: 0171 840 8400; Fax: 0171 834 2509.
For a FREE Methuen Drama catalogue please contact Methuen Drama
at the above address.